Four Seasons of Emotions
Poems for the bleeding heart

Tony Gugel

Four Seasons of Poetry:
Poetry for the Bleeding Heart

Copyright © 2025 by Tony Gugel. All rights reserved. This book or any portion thereof may not be reproduced or used in any manner whatsoever without the express written permission except in the case of reprints in the context of reviews.

Cover design by Tony Gugel

ISBN: 979-8-218-60599-5

Dedications

I want to express my deepest thanks to everyone who has ever sparked emotion within me. To those few with whom I first shared my poems — thank you. It isn't easy to open up and share raw emotions, but I am fortunate and blessed to have such incredible and supportive friends who saw me through my vulnerability with open hearts. You have been my anchor through lifes storms which I might not have always made it though.
        There are many moments of highs and lows with which this collection would not exist. I'm sorry for the times I withdrew into my darker seasons, writing has been my way of navigating those shadows and though I may not have always been present, know that I love you all and had thought and still think of you often.

Thank you for being part of this journey. This book, and these poems, would not have been possible without you.

And to my dog, Zelda, without whom I wouldn't have a reason to get up in the morning.

Everything In Its Season

Fall... 7

Winter... 61

Spring.. 135

Summer....................................... 207

Fall

Alone, Loss, Heartbreak

--Puzzle of Heart Break

The separation of one heart into two
Where two half's made a whole
And a hole is where a piece goes missing
The box once full now empty.
Dumped on the table to find what was once there.
The puzzle being not did they fit, but where did the last piece go?

--Your opinion

I want your opinion
I value your mind
So why don't you answer
Why can't you find
That I can be more than your distractions
Put down your phone
Can't your chats wait?
Our time is limited and precious
I'm sorry I'm upset, I don't wanna use this tone
But soon we won't be here
Because you'll have moved on

--Don't go

I can't stand this stress anymore
Suffocating here on this floor
Hoping, waiting for you to come through that door
Because I can't breathe without you
You breathe life in me
I would die without you can't you see
I need you here
Here with me
Please don't go

--Eclipse of the heart

Little did he know that when the moon eclipsed the sun it wasn't a sign to give his heart away, it wasn't the time arrived and planets aligned
It was a sign to shield his heart from things to come
The way the moon shielded the earth from the sun
Now he thought;
Now should he see such beauty again
If the stars fell in a shower of meteors like the sky was falling, should he cry?
Cry like the rain
If the seasons changed in his fall to winter should his heart turn cold?
When will he see his sign and learn from the universe that even in the spring he to might again bloom and grow
That here on earth hearts can heal
That even in the dark there is a little light and in the dawn there is a new day

--Be still my heart

Be still my heart
Be still my mind
I know that I will soon be fine
I tremble, shake, the thought of you
A love now lost, to be one not two
I lay here now, beside my bed
Thoughts of you inside my head

--The Seed I'll never know

I waited so long for you, my waiting that will never be.
The seed never planted, the seed I'll never see.
I hoped so long, to see you happy
That you would come to me if you were sad.
We would reminisce on memories, to laugh in times gone mad.
One day you'd to grow big and strong, to be wise beyond your years.
Even if you didn't need me, I'd still be here, to wipe away your fears.
I dreamed for everyday I held you close, to never let you go.
I selfishly thought you would be only mine alone, but no one would ever know
An image I held to tightly, and may now have to let go.
I'm sorry, to you, for me.
My thought that will never be
The seed I'll never know.

--Broken Futures in the Multiverse of Madness

Broken futures and things I'll never see
What ifs and imaginings are fracturing me
Multiverse of madness I'll never know
Times and spaces I'll never go
I've tried to change I really have
I just can't seem to find the path
With broken dreams and failed attempts
Over and over and I've given up since
Where would I go, who would I be
If somewhere in the multiverse I found a happier me

--My life is crashing down around me

As my life is crashing down around me
I built it up with no where to go
I, a castle
Love you, but I'm on the ledge
Just let me hold on a little longer
Crumbling, as I fall apart
So don't let go

As you walk out that door
Family emblem lying on the floor
Will you keep my name
Etched on your heart
As mine slowly falls apart
There is no more you and no more us
Armor and weapons made of steel, left to rust
And if you leave it might be the last thing
I might feel

--On this post

On this post, I post what's real
Because that's the way I truly feel
I don't mean to sound so rude
But if I'm in a saddened mood
Help me out and raise my spirit
For if you don't you might well fear it
I'll continue down this road I swear it
If you don't like it you'll have to deal
My emotions now like a spinning wheel
Don't know how I'll feel next
I'll leave you feeling truly vexed
For I will only spit the truth
So get me off this road called ruth

--Shadows in my eye

I look to the room, the wall, the corner
Something has changed, but I don't know what, how or why
Everything in its place, nothing amiss
Yet, what is this filter before my eyes?
Everything a new shade of dark
A cover of shadows that wasn't there
But from what?
It's silent here
What is this dimness in the world around me and will it ever go away?
From what was once vibrant and bright
What has changed… And why?

--Ghost of missing you

Imagination of thing's not there
Of seeing you, when you're not here
Wishing, missing
Try not to care
A thought I crave still to hold
To feel the warmth that's turned to cold
Thoughts turned wild, mild and then
In the gentle thrashing of the night
My heart cry's for the memories of what was once there
A ghost of missing you

--Parting Memories

When paths part ways
And what was built is razed
Hearts will ache
And ships will break
Memories held will last forever
Despite our thoughts and best endeavors
Some things are not meant to last
And time always seems to go by to fast
I wish the best
And now lay to rest
To what once was and always will be
My favorite times and memories

--I lost my way

I've lost the map
I can't find the stars
Can't find the planets
Or guiding mars
I've lost my compass
Nothing looks the same
My Memory's fading
The trail that I took, the rains washed away
I've lost my guide, to life's big adventure
Where have you gone?
Without you, I lost my way home

--If I could tell you everything

Titled words and unfinished poems
Like crumbled thrones falling apart
Minds lost like kings gone mad
Wandering, wondering, lost
Searching, but never finding
Words like people, where did they go?
In my silence I want to scream them out, but the words stick in my throat
Choking on the little death taking over
As castles crumble, burn them to the ground like pages in the fire
Watch as the last words fade away
So much to say, but now I'm gone
Run away, for I am the king of nothing
I bow to the throne of empty and lost words
Things left unsaid
And out of everything, I wish I could tell you about…

--Scream to the wind

We scream to the wind, we can't be heard
I shout to the void, where I make no sound
I wail to the ocean, that she might wave goodbye
I curse the fate, whose path can be cruel
I cry to the desert, where I make no tears
I bury the soul to the grave,
That flowers might bloom

--What if it was Me

What if instead of you being the one that died it was me
And by letting go of life you had lived
What if by living I have died
By continuing to live I die a little bit each day
With my heart continuously breaking
I am a ghost wandering lost each day
By continuing to live I am trapped in this purgatory, forgotten
While you are free, missed and remembered every day.
What if you were the one that lived and I was the ghost.

--Another day alone

I have lost track of the nights
Time
Eternities
The fathomless voids of nothingness
Were nothing happens.
Alone in the dark where all there is, is the silence and the beating of my own heart
And even that has lost the rhythm of time
What day is it?
Has it been that long since I've gotten to interact with another soul?
This rock in my hand makes no sound as I wait for it to ring
The weight of it growing heavier as the world grows dim
I wish to scream just to break the silence, but I can't make a sound
Why is the world outside so quiet?
Has it really only been a day?
I've lost track of the eternities

--Why is it I feel this way

Why is it I feel this way, I think about you almost everyday
I try to deny the way I feel, I fear these wounds will never heal
Because I know now that you don't care, you played with my heart, that wasn't fair
I have issues, yeah that much is true, but was it so wrong for me to fall for you
All I wanted was just one chance, to experience love and romance
I'm angry now, but not at you, I hate myself for the thoughts ensued
So don't judge me, I can't help the way I feel
Because to me, these thoughts are real

--I don't understand

I don't understand
Because I don't listen
I see through your lies
Giving me double vision
I try to stay silent
To keep my mind closed
But defiant it goes
And nobody knows
The pain inside
The wound you left exposed
To trust you again
Would be a mistake
Because now I know
That your truth is fake
Why did you lie?

--Holding back Love

When love is to easily slipped
What is love in a world when it isn't love anymore?
When it is to easily said as it glides off the tongue
But what does it mean when you hold it back
Weigh it down so it doesn't crush and hurt someone
Tie it down and crucify it
You hurt yourself before they hurt you
Yet there it is
In your attempt to hide it
It's hung up for all the world to see

--Spring

Spring
Came and you brought me into the world
In Summer
You showed me the golden sun and how to grow
In the Fall
The storms came and washed you away
In Winter
I was left to pick up the pieces alone in the cold

--So long

Its been so long since I've seen you now and I don't know what to say
I don't always show it, but I've missed you everyday
We've suffered for so long, from this burning pain inside
You chose to blow out your candle
I chose to let mine burn
My candle may be shorter, but its flames lived longer now
My heart feels like shattered clay
Your memory like melting wax in the sun
I don't even know you, the person that you were
All I see is the still images in the frame
All I hear are the whispers in the wind
All I taste is my cries in the night
And all I feel is nothing
Because I never got to know you, yet I still love you
From your wax I took shape, from your flame I was born
Yet you still chose to blow out your candle
And I chose to live
I may not always be happy, but
I'm Alive

--Iron maiden of the heart

Iron Maiden of the heart
As the casket slowly closes
I wonder why the tin man wanted a heart
As the spikes slowly push forth
I look out the visor of my eyes
And watch the blood pour out
As she locks the lid I see the light
And wonder
Am I the tin man?

--I sit here in this empty room

I sit alone and drink my tea
For soon I know that I will be
Asleep in bed, beneath the sea
I hope to find that rusty key
Unlock the door to set me free
A hope, a prayer, a silent plea
Alone, alone, I no longer see
The possibility, of you here at home, with me

--Life inside this empty room

I sit here in this empty room
All these thoughts they seal my doom
I cannot run, I cannot hide
These feelings I have locked inside
I sit here wait for hope to come
To save me from myself

--Prison house

Trapped in a silent world
4 walls, ceiling and floor
Plenty of windows and a few doors
But there is no escape
Do people still exist out there?
I count the days of my self incarceration
I could leave any time, but where would I go
No money to stay, non to go
So I repeat
Is anyone out there?
I'm all alone

--Reverberations of silence

The reverberations of silence echo hauntingly against my soul
This house a prison cell of my mind as the earth shattering silence halts time
Even the tick tock of the clock and the creak of the floor boards are quiet in the vacant halls
Heart beats loud as drums of war fighting back the emptiness in my ear
As the hum of silence continues to pierce the night
Silently I scream as I struggle for breath
Chest burning as the drum beats louder
Tears stream like rivers of blood in a never ending war
If only there was another presence to pierce the veil of silence
But all I hear is ghosts and echoes

--Bad dreams & Nightscapes

Bad dreams and nightscapes
Trapped minds with no escapes
Labyrinths with giant beasts
Horned demons who like to feast
I've lost you, I've lost my mind
Searching deep to try and find
Let me out, take me away
There's no escape night or day
Caught in a web cast by the fay
But is it fate that's kept me locked up
that makes me stay
Let me out this nightmare dream
I'll pay the jailer, don't make me scream
Silent sound I wish you'd hear
But the demons have found me I fear
So I make no sound and try to disappear
They grab my heart and tear me down
My souls been torn up, thrown around
Cast aside far and near
Not much left of what was here
My missing pieces you might have found
Please take note upon the ground, my mind, my labyrinth, has been my hell
There is no escape from this prison cell
I'm a ghost of what I once was
A demon feasting
And I'm not safe from myself

— Restless sleep

Who am I supposed to talk to at midnight when I can't sleep
Who will hold me back from my doubts and save me from myself
Who's hand am I supposed to hold at 2 am when the demons in my head won't stop their incessant whispers
Who will hold my head in there hands, shield my ears, replacing the whispers with their own while placing a kiss upon my forehead
As I restlessly try to sleep and time passes to quickly in the night
I am alone in a world full of ghosts as no one can always be there in my time of need as time blows them away, as memories drift in the night and there's no one to hold

--Instability

Insanity
It's clear to me
That of which I am
Part of the broken an the damned
But no one even notices as I walk on by
The pain and suffering in my soul, as I cover up my eyes

--No rest for the Wicked

They say there's no rest for the wicked
Perhaps it's my wicked mind taking over me
Evil thoughts taking over, stick around long enough maybe you will see
The evils I keep behind locked door
I try to blind the evil eye, look not into my eyes for fear of what you might see
My wicked heart will brandish the knife, with cuts so deep only I can bleed
Kill my thoughts and my heart at the bottom
Corrupt to the core with these evils inside of me
Acting against what is considered good and right

--Satellite

As I float among the stars
I'm destined not to touch
I see the paths of the ones before
I look to the paths I crossed
Choices not mine
I tire of drifting like a satellite
I will drift into a dark sun
I bow to fate

As a human satellite
I drift among the stars I'm destined to never touch
Can they hear my voice in the vacuum of space?
No choice in the path as I'm pulled into the void
As I fight to breathe air
Cursed to drift alone
I fade to the dark sun
And bow to fate

--Melancholy sadness

Melancholy sadness for a soul so sad
Drifting in a day that was not that bad
Distance between us
Can you feel me looking out?
Through time and space
Searching for a light in the dark
Have I drifted to far
Fading out
In the rain of the night and clouds in the mind
Where do I go, where should I be?
How do I find you? Are you waiting there for me?
I'm lost in this world, is there no escape?
I can't help but wonder
Is this destiny or fate?

--I thought that I was over you

I thought that I was over you
Your bright smile, your eyes of hue
You hurt me once you know it's true
And my thoughts turned so blue
In the end I finally knew
You didn't care, you used me too
You lead me on, because you knew
I was alone, I wouldn't know
I couldn't handle the emotion any more
So I went inside and locked the door

--Whispers

Sweet whispers you used to put into my ear
To ease the rising storm
Each caress a lapping wave to settle my heart
Rocking back and forth till it is eased to slumber

--Ever since

Ever since this broken heart, I don't know where to start
Ever since we've been apart I just haven't been me
Every single morning I've been waking up alone the weight of the world on my shoulders feels like it has grown
I try to lift it up, I try to move along, but this rock is crushing me in the place where I had once had flown. Ever since this broken heart I just haven't been me.

I spend time with my family, oh but they don't understand. How lonely they have made me, how sad that I have been. I try to keep a smile on and try to keep it in.

I hang out with my friends and I try to hide my feelings, I try to hide the truth. The sadness, grief and jealousy, I didn't have in youth. I think I have a problem, there's got to be a way. To go back to who I was and get myself to stay.
Ever since this broken heart, I look into the mirror, I look into my eyes and I see that it's not me.

--Surrounded and alone

Surrounded by people
Yet I couldn't feel more alone
Can they see it
Please don't look into my eyes
I don't want to give it away
Could I ever find comfort in strangers?
A heart to touch
I reach out, only to retract
Snapping back to the sting of the whip
I could float away in this pain
Someone, please hold me before I disappear
So I don't feel more alone

--I try to hide

I try to hide
This pain inside
But I'm failing, falling
My thoughts mauling
Me from the inside out
I have no strength
I'm crawling
As I scream and shout
I turn to a whisper
But you can't hear me out
So all my hope turns to doubt
But you don't seem to care
And I fear I won't be found
As I die here on the ground

--Shield Sister

Shield sister
My sister in arms
We protect each other from things that would harm
Hold me close
Run not away
Tell me yet, that you wish to stay
The monster within, longs to take over
With the demons call and I fear I will fall
My hope, my shield are nothing at all and they have both become so splintered.
This battle field could soon be cindered
To my dismay, have I been forgotten?
Without you at my back I'm sure to lose this day
Is it true? The demons say you have turned away
Is that your shield that faces my direction?
With my face in its reflection?
Please don't abandon me to me
I shield my heart and you from myself, but I never thought I would have to shield myself from you.

--Fighting demons inside my head

Fighting demons inside my head
My mind and body filled with dread
These thoughts that I can no longer bare
When life no longer seeming fair
What is it that I can do
But lay here alone
Without you

--Broken and Breaking

Broken and breaking
All the times I've been told it'll get better
In my doubts I tell you it doesn't matter
Scars I left from all the nights I was left alone
As nothing ever changes
And all I ever want is what I can't have
As I'm left to wander this world alone
To put more scars upon my heart

--Insanity

I feel myself slipping away
Every night and every day
I try to hold on, to the way I was
I fear what I'll become because
The thoughts, the demons, I know there plan
They say that they will destroy this man
I try to turn to run away
They tie me down and make me stay
The demons inherited from the one before
She didn't survive, she lives no more
Ten years have past and the wound not healed
The emotions I didn't understand, kept locked and sealed
Alone I broke, and when I spoke
I lost all control, the tears inside came crashing down
Dead, alone I was found
With my thoughts and my demons
I am alone, it's only me
And my insanity

--paranoid

I've become paranoid as I try to avoid
These thoughts and these feelings that lie in my head
And I know that I should get some sleep and go to bed
But I can't sleep any more, what's the point, what is it for
And I'm starting to hear and see things that weren't there before
And I can no longer ignore the fear
From this torturous pain, a lasting nightmare
And I need help from someone to save me from myself
But they don't even care, like they forgot me on a shelf
But I'm endanger from my insanity
But it's only me, it doesn't matter
I'm just paranoid
I've been alone for so long maybe it's them I'm trying to avoid

--Emotions rise emotions fall

Emotions Rise, emotions fall
My heart will never hear the call
Of Love not lost and never found
Running away from homeward bound

--Broken heart, weight of mortality

I'm beginning to feel the weight of my own mortality
I'm drowning in myself
I feel the weight of this broken heart
And I'm taking on water
Hearts still beating, but it's fading fast
I need your touch, God bring me back
I feel it in my lonely soul
The hole inside
The beating of my heart
The weight of my mortality
I'm drowning in myself

--Innocence of Icarus

Like Icarus, my emotions flew high
I tried to touch the stars
Hands outstretched
My wings melted
Falling, I lost my halo
The innocence of youth

--I'm afraid I'll always be alone

I'm afraid I will always be alone
When it comes to love what have I done wrong?
I wait and I wait and no one comes along
As the years pass by 1, 2 then 3
Why is it I'm still at the end of the line and no one's picked me
I'm wandering though life thinking it's not fair, I see all the couples as they run off in pairs
Off into the sunset where no one can see
Me by myself, alone as can be

I don't want anything magnificent and grand
Just something simple, thoughtful and unplanned
The most underrated things a couple can do
A hug so tight I can feel it in my soul too
A wonderful hand for mine to hold
To stay up all night and talk about life

But I'm afraid my heart has been cut by a knife
It's been so long, I fear what they might say
Damaged and broken
There's probably no hope left for him anyway

--The wolf

The Wolf
Howls at the moon
He's watching, waiting, hoping soon
Plain as day, black as night
Seeing him, the saddest sight
All alone, he tries to fight
The thoughts, his mind, with all his might
He stands his ground and shakes his head
For inside, he is, nearly dead
He's always been,
He'll always be
The lone wolf alone
Inside of me

--Fade away

Family, friends they fade away
The memories are there to stay
Try to forget, I wish I could
Ignorant bliss, in the days I stood
Way up high and to the sky
I looked and looked, one day asked why
I felt alone among the stars
Off alone by distant mars
I tried to find my way back home
But couldn't find a map, a poem, or song
A life alone I shall remain
My life was lived alone in vain

They all pair up, two by two
And when they ask where are you
Alone I answer, but what else is new
Among the few that never knew
How to fight for love they knew was true
Feelings not returned, turn blue
Eventually I shied away from you
And in the end I finally knew
Emotions end, the final blow
I died in no ones arms, and now you know

Sometimes you have to go through hell to get to heaven

--hallow home

Hollow shell that was once a home
Through the halls I wander and roam
Haunting this place like a memory
Of all the things that couldn't be
Hallow shell that was once a heart
Shattered broken fell apart
A stained glass window, sun once shown through
Boarded up with no clue
Of a
Hallow shell that was that was once a soul
Lies a lump, less than coal
By the hearth it burned to bright
A dust of ash is all that remains
To be blown away should the door be opened again.

--Now what

Now what
Left here with all that was never done or said
All done for love that was it just a dream
I close my eyes and stand on the edge
Empty house not a home
With a heart left unchecked and left to roam

Winter

Anger, Depression, Sleep

--What is anger

What is anger
Anger is the shackle, fresh from the demon's forge that binds us to our rage.
The blindfold over our eyes to the destruction as they whisper lies in your ears. But don't try to reply, for as soon as you open your mouth, they will place the coals, hot from the fire down your throat till your screaming voice is raw with the splinters. Holding onto anger is like holding hot blades. While we can hurt those around us in our fury, we burn ourselves as well. May we one day fight the demons inside us. Use the forge to make a key to free us from our senseless rage. Remove the blinds that bind us. Hold back and think before we speak. And let go of the blades that burn us and cut down others.

--Who am I mad at

Who am I mad at, I don't even know. Is it me, No, its you
Because you don't even know what you put me through
But even if you do, you don't even care
One minute you where there, the next you're gone
And now you just expect me to go and move on
Ya I might be emotional, I am depressed
From all the emotions that I have repressed
But I think its time I confessed
I've thought about ending it all
Jump off the edge, you're watching me fall
Because when I needed help, you ignored my call

You lied when you said you cared
Instead I'll die and all you can say is good bye
And you made me feel so dumb
Leaving me to feel so numb
I went for a walk in the snow to see if I would freeze
I don't think this pain will ever be eased

My hearts turned cold
I live with the cards I've been dealt
Living with all the feelings I've felt
But tonight I think that I'll fold

— Isolation

8:32am
I have plenty of time
I brush my hair
Made breakfast
I take a walk
Clean the house
Fix the wall
Do some writing
The list is done
    Hours go by
    There's nowhere to go
    I don't want to be a bother
    So I wait by the phone
    No one to talk to
    The house is to quiet
    I haven't eaten
    I stare at a blank wall
Days go by
I have to much time
Things I once did bring no joy
The phone is to quiet
I pull my out my hair
The silence is deafening
I still haven't eaten
I place a hole in the wall
The house is to quiet
I scream and nobody hears it
    I haven't heard from anyone in weeks
    I can't sleep
    I'm not hungry
    Shaved my head
    My world is to quiet
    My thoughts are to loud
    Messages unread
    What time is it?
    What day?
    Each moment is an eternity
    Not a sound from the phone
    No presence I'm all alone
    I haven't heard from anyone
    And it's only
8:33am

--Let it be known

Let it be known that I give up
That I no longer give a f**k
For try and try and try again
I've always lost in the end
For when I tried and failed some more
It re-flamed a battle, a raging war
Between my heart, my mind and soul
An endless chasm I did fall
Into the darkest part of mind
Sadness, anger did I find
And among them ever more
Like pages of a book I ripped and tore
And threw them out forever more
I do not want to see them again
I'll stay here alone in my dark den

I no longer have control
My mind, my body or my soul

--Comfortable floor

It's been months since I've slept on a bed
I've bin sleeping on the ground
How does that sound
It's more comfortable, when I wake up, I feel more stable
Like I was born in a barn, the life I live, my story a fable
And all I ever wanted was a happy ending, but my patience is pending

--Tears on the pillow

Tears on the pillow
As I pretend to be ok
I fear there is no change
That it will always be this way
They say you can't predict what tomorrow brings
But I'm afraid I can when every day is the same
It ends every night with me and my bleeding heart in my hand

--Another day

Another day, a night, alone
Not a sound from the phone
But it's ok, I don't have much to say
Why would i burden you with my thoughts that way

Everything's to quiet for the voices in my head
They tend to get louder when I'm trying to go to bed
The demons deep inside me wishing to be fed
Eating me alive and I'm wishing I was dead

I'm stuck in this room and I'm drowning all alone
My head is a prison cell and this house is not a home
my friends always tell me to just pick up the phone

But I'm lost ok. And I can't get your attention.
I open my mouth and you turn away at the mention.
My depression is flaring as people seem to stop caring. I'm left alone in this world with the one thing I fear
As everyone walks away and I disappear

When I die don't cry for me
Don't waste you water on this dessert, as my emotions have run dry
You never cried for me when I was living why would you now
Easily forgotten, left alone when I fell down
When I die
Don't cry for me when you didn't cry before

I'm not afraid to die, not anymore
I'm afraid to be left alone with my thoughts
To be miss understood
I'll walk away this time, perhaps this time for good

Does it scare you when I talk about dying?
Why when it's already like I'm not even there

Just existing till the end with this life that isn't living
When it feels like nobody is there that cared

-- Decoration friend

A background wall in every picture
The best that I can hope for, is to be a permanent fixture
Easily forgotten, the last to know
What's going on, did you want to go?
You ask me to go and I don't understand why
Am I just a friend filler in your eyes
I go along, but do I belong
I feel so awkward, but I might be wrong
I try to remember that this is my friend
I try to smile along and try to pretend
to hold to the thought that I belong
but in my fear and doubt that steers me wrong
So I stay real quiet, I don't make a sound
I'm a decoration friend hidden in the background

--Broken Futures

Broken futures
Hopes of the past
Was it never meant to last
Dreams of the future
Planning never paid off and time passed
Try to hold onto you
Life left scars that slowly grew
In you
You let go of what was meant to be
To surviving on your knees
Pleading, please
Don't let them suffer too
Times change and we do too
But it was never meant to be you
You had such bright beginnings
The lights dimmed a little,
Have we really changed so much?
Is it true?
My heart is breaking, broken
Changes and fractures
Barely holding ourselves together
Changes in our statures
Seeing all these broken futures

--My New December

Thank you for another month to remember
This my pain, My new December
There is no more rain, just drifting snow
Covering a freezing heart that's cracked, broke and slow
My trust was shattered like brittle ice
The shards of memory, they cut and dice
Another reason to feel cold and alone
Left to realize what I need to face on my own
For some there is no forever
Icy jewels melt from what was once thought to be treasure
Bones are numb and I feel no more
Pain tingling of what is and isn't brushed through my core
I know not what I face, but the blistering wind has frozen tears in my disgrace
Another memory to burn in the cold
The pain of a memory I don't want to hold
I don't want to remember
This my pain, My new December
May it be wiped away like footprints in the snowy breeze
May it be wiped away before I freeze
But even if I thaw my pain might never fully ease

--World of Negativity

How do I stand up to the weight of the world
When it places all it's burdens on your shoulder
When it's crushing weight makes you want to step aside and remove yourself from its presence
When all you want is to know and see is positivity, but everyone and everything come at you with negativity and complaints
How do you hold onto the good, when the world has you spinning around till you fall
Drowning in a pool negativity and doubt
How can people say they want to live in a world of happiness and hope when their very words bring down the ones around them

--Overthinker

Mind in past is set to race
Time sets to a slower pace
Repeat, repeat a thousand times
Many thoughts, a thousand different lines
I cannot escape temptation and wonder
The thoughts I tend to scrutinize and ponder
To overthink the fate of the world
Should I, shouldn't I, as it all unfurled
Could I have just made it all a little different?
My heart split and incoherent
Mind and heart fight away
Past, present, future paralyzed by day
Frozen by night, my mind, my mind I try to fight
My mind is scrambled and I'm in shambles
I think and think it never goes away
Past, future, present thoughts I can't make stay
I try to plan the future today
But I cannot change the past away
My mind is split, my heart is broken
Are my thoughts better left unspoken?
My overthinking is driving me insane
Past, present, future, heart and mind are all in pain.

--Wasted time

Waste of time, waste of life
Mind as blank as this screen I lay before
Head on the floor, hand outstretched to the ceiling
I want to *scream* to the universe

***What am I supposed to do*?!?**

--This useless feeling

This useless feeling
With which I'm dealing
I no longer stand to bare
Emotions try to run amuck,
And life just seems unfair
I want to help, the way I felt
The thoughts I wish to share
I don't know how
To express or show
That all I do is care

--Will I ever be able to sleep

Will I ever be able to sleep
Or will I always be haunted by these demons inside my head,
Every night I lay in my bed, and think about the things I've done and the words I said
I wonder how I'm still alive, why I'm not dead
And I tell myself I don't care that life isn't fair, I look to the ceiling an all I can do is just stare, At the shadows that live there, but they don't even know, they don't even care about
What I should do or where I should go
I let my self get sad, then angry, till I say no
The mixed emotions that I kept locked up, I lost my control
And I just let them flow
Like tears streaming down, like a river running away,
I got lost and I found, I fell to the ground
That I couldn't let myself be this way any more
I don't even know what I was really angry for
I was turning in to something I'm not,
I realized I was turning it my mother, but in time I caught
Myself before the end, because in the end she was dead
She made her own bed, when all is said and done
I'm still alive, I'm a survivor
For those who know me, know I not a liar
I do what I say and I say what I do
I have to survive, I'll do it for you

--Starving love

Starving for truth
Starving for my own love story
You're so far away
Don't leave me all alone
I don't know who you are but I'm falling

--Falling heart

God save me because I'm falling
And my soul can't afford to be falling in love
I reach for the stars, they're crashing around me
This meteor stuck me in the heart

--Remove my heart

I want it removed
I want open heart surgery
My heart is eternally broken
It's always bleeding
Can't you see the pieces?
I don't want to feel the pain of these sharp jaded feelings anymore
Every time I fall it breaks a little more
Glass turned to sand in an hour glass of time
And the more I wait for things to change
The more I feel the weight
Cutting deeper into the scars that won't seem to heal
My heart hurts and all I want is to scream how much I love you
But I can't, so I swallow the pain and wait for numbness that'll never come

--I, like my mind, wander too

I, like my mind, wander too
It seems to wander right to you
I don't know why, I wish I knew
What is it I'm supposed to do

--I bow to fate

As I await the next blow of fate
a choice I make
Do I face everything and rise
Or do I except defeat
As I'm kicked down to my knees
I bow to fate

--Broken Vacuum

Every day you try to survive
With the fake smiles you try to hide behind
Waiting for the excitement of being in a room
Sitting in the corner like a boring vacuum waiting to be used
But it could be days or even weeks before your needed again
Each passing moment is so quiet in your head
But what happens if you were no longer around
If they plugged you in and you didn't work hard enough anymore
Broken down on the floor
And you feel like you'd be better off on the curb dead and replaced

--G.r.i.n.d

I am no more than a cog in a machine
Tired and worn
Ready to be discarded at any moment
I am life
An ant on a hill
I am a dreamer of dreams
Waiting on change

Get
Ready
It's a
New
Day

--Feelings of Jealousy and greed

Jealousy and greed
Selfishness of want and need
I hate that I feel this way, it isn't right, my thoughts of sin, when I should pray
For these thoughts to go away
For to crave for what you can't have
To take it all, like it's up for grabs
Bury the feeling, I'm feeling torn
The thread of what makes me, becoming worn
You can't have what was never yours
The heart I crave to love is yours
Like vampiric blood was spilt on you
The beast inside I wish you knew
I'm a dragon and you're my horde
I'm the king and your lord
Do as I say, you're my siren song
Have I succumb to jealousy and greed? Where did I go wrong?
Steer the ship, my emotions away
I cannot let these feelings stay
Run, please run, run away
Have I become a blood thirst demon?
Or some kind of barbaric heathen?
I try to be remain a gentleman
Or am I just another stupid human

--Silent Screams

There's a scream inside my head
It gets louder as I go to bed
It echos through me, to my bones
A tuning fork when I'll I wanted to be a rose
This bleeding hearts been pricked by thorns
And now I can't stop bleeding out
Can you hear me now?

There's a scream inside me, am I quiet or can you hear it echoing
I see the blood, my heart feels empty
Foot steps in chambers of my heart
I can see the light at the end of the tunnel
But I'm afraid it might be to far

I walk a lonely road, so broken and so cold
I can't stand the sight of me, my reflections echoing
Broken smiles cracked in glass
I try to hide behind a broken mask
But I hear it echoing like a silent drum that makes me scream
Am I quiet or can you hear the echoing?

There's a scream inside me, am I quiet or can you hear it echoing
I see the blood, my heart feels empty
Foot steps in chambers of my heart
I can see the light at the end of the tunnel
But I'm afraid it might be to far

I'm screaming now can you hear it echo
Your the light at the end of the tunnel
But you were to far from the start
I'm bleeding out and don't think I'll make it
Shattered dreams and echos of a broken heart

I see the blood, my heart feels empty. There's a scream inside, am I quiet or can you hear it echoing

--Creature of Habit

I am nothing if not a creature of habit
Repeating events and tasks day after day
Habitual thoughts to my dismay
I stay in my cave, my cavern, my den
Occasionally, I'll wander out every now and again
But nothing ever truly changes, I'll go though the motions, the phases, the stages
Occasionally, you could get me to talk and to speak
I'll tell you I'm doing something different, unique
But the truth is everything is always the same
And I have no one, but myself to blame.
At the end of the day, I'm just trying to survive
I lie I'm my room waiting for the one to arrive
To take me away, perhaps second hand change
As I watch the clock on the wall, isn't it strange
How this creature of habit, this beast inside
Is so desperate to be fed change
It's eating me alive, but I don't have the currency to pay for it's meal
I'm terrified, I feel I'm willing to make a really bad deal
If I sit and I wait perhaps it will change, make believe it all isn't real
This creature of habit can't stay forever the same
But if I don't make it out alive, I have no one else but myself to blame
I'm cursed in my ways, a creature of habit
I put myself here, this is my fault
And if I don't make a change, I fear the result

--Loud thoughts

Thoughts, thoughts
So loud and clear
Doubts, distrust, silence, fear
Louder, louder around they go
Screaming, scary, carnival
Where's the keys? minds displaced
I have to escape this maddening place
What do I do?
Where do I go?
The thoughts, the thoughts
They spin me around
Screaming, screaming
Someone please help
The noise, it's to loud
The flashing, I'm crashing, I'm falling down
Life's getting to hard to move forward
With shoes of a sad clown

--Picking up the pieces

Thoughts, thoughts
Dangerous and loud
Cannot be held and or bound
Thoughts like fires spit and they burn
Swift is the fire, dry kindling in the wind
Times sand turns to glass
And shatters to the ground
Fragmented shards, jagged and jaded
Who in the crowd will be left?
With bloody palms
To pick up the pieces

--Who was there

These thoughts, these thoughts
They have become so loud
I no longer hear your voice
Drowned in the crowd
Lost and alone
shattered and trampled
I pick up the pieces
Cuts from the sharp edges
After the sun sets
Who was there?

--I want to disappear

I want to fade into the background and disappear
Go back to a place where no one knows me there
To be silent in my suffering
In my disease I want to be enveloped by the darkness and fed upon by my demons
Let them pick their teeth with my bones
I no longer care
As long as I am numb from the pain and the chaos in my mind is hidden behind the clouds
The rain will wash away the blood and soon enough I will be forgotten just like every other day.
It doesn't even matter whether go or if I stay
Life has never been fair, and I don't expect it to be.
I don't even expect for a little mercy from the pain in the numbness in me
Just another scar on an otherwise useless ugly soul
So in the night I'll just slip away
I'll fade into the background and disappear

--My friends say

My friends say I deserve to be happy, but I don't understand
I haven't done anything I don't deserve that view
I look in the mirror and think how can it be true
You deserve to be happy?
How can anyone love you?

--I don't want to be alone

I don't wanna be alone any more
Lying down here on the bathroom floor
I don't wanna have to cry
But it's just another day, where I want to die
The devil in the mirror looks back with cold dead eyes, saying I won't survive
What if this is the way it's supposed to be
Climbing out the mirror he's gonna murder me

I'm trapped, in my mind
If I opened up, what would you find?
Death and destruction
Or Hope in a pit trying to survive

--Gaze of your eyes

If I looked into your eyes could I resist your gaze
Would my choices be my own or would it be a mistake
If you had me in your arms could I resist the temptation of your lips
The dazzling gleam of your smile
The speech of your tongue could make me melt in your hands
I can only imagine the depth of your soul
As I look into your eyes
I don't wish to taint your light
With my darkness

--don't open, dead inside

I am unbelievably aware of the pounding in my chest
The emotions I keep locked up there
Pounding on the door
Waiting, bursting to get out

But I can't because it'll kill me

--Wake me up

Wake me up
I've fallen into the dream turned nightmare
I'm wide awake, but it's like I'm sleepwalking
I'm moving slow
Motions slowed
Muscles atrophied
I can hardly move
Life is smothering me
I can't wake up
Dreams within dreams
As days change to nights
How do I fight the predetermined path
Subconscious inception
Trapped within my mind
Take my hand and pull me out
Overthinking and overwhelmed
I may be alive
But it's like I'm sleepwalking

--I'm okay

I'm okay, I'm okay
Is that just something I say?
When everything begins and ends the same way each and every day
I hold onto myself, holding back my emotions
But I'm losing my grip and all of my devotions
Everything I once loved feels lost, the joy has gone away
Everything I thought I had was never meant to stay
I am not okay
And every day I fall to my knees and pray
Please dear God I was happy once, please don't take that away
What is this punishment? What did I do that was so bad?
I'm screaming to the empty sky, looking for a sign of change while slowly going mad
I'm okay, I'm okay
I tell myself each and every day
I have to tell myself this, that it has to be this way.
That I'm meant to be alone, my friends so far away. They get to go off and play while I'm stuck at home and stay

--Killing heart

Murder on the stage
Serial killer on the loose
Getting away for years
Has life lost all meaning?
You may spark the feeling
But I'll smother the flame
I'll walk away
Silent as the night
Because I know you'll never feel the same
I've gotten really good at killing my heart

--Missing

Place a picture on a milk carton
Send for the police
Call out the news
Alert the media and phone every line
It's a terrible tragedy

I have gone missing
And nobody knows

--It will take time to get over you

It will take time to get over you
Because you're like a long winding road
And I got lost in your eyes,
Filled with sky's of blue
But I didn't see the storm
Where I got stuck, I got struck
Like lightning, the feeling almost took my life away
My heart almost stopped when I looked at you
I was paralyzed, and
It will take time to get over you

--Destructive Nature

You gave me destructive nature
You brewed a storm
My Mind is clouded by the
Smoke from fire formed
Fear my power
That no one may be harmed

--Stained Glass Heart

Stained glass heart
What was once vibrant and strong
Lie broken on the ground
Shards of Glass jagged and sharp
May one day an artisan carefully pick up the pieces
And place them back into the mosaic of your life
That a spectrum of light might shine once more on your
beautiful soul

--Glass windows of the soul

Sadness drips from the glass windows of the soul. Eyes overwhelmed from the pain of the world and the pain from within. But look not to other windows for fear of judgment if the glass might shatter.

--What If

What if it was all a lie
What it were never meant to come true
What if I'm not good enough
What if I can't survive
What if I never know what it's like to breath again
What if I can't be happy
What if the pain is permanent
What if everything I ever wanted was all I ever needed
What if what I needed wasn't what I wanted anymore

--I have a Dark Feeling

I have a dark feeling, I'm going to die
I look to the ceiling and the sky
I talk to the room, I wish on the stars
I sing the lyrics to counting blue cars
I don't know where to go, my hearts covered in scars
I beg and I plead, am I really that far?
Life in this house
I cling to loose hope
I'm hanging by a moment
I hang by a thread
I survive each day
But I'm not living, but undead
Lost and alone, trapped in my mind
The one in the mirror is often unkind
Feed my soul, I'm starving for truth
In the sky of a million stars
What is one more light gone out?
In my dark feeling, in the face of my demons
I hold to the creed
Is 6 feet really that far?
Will my soul ever be freed?

--A Warning from My Demons

There's a warning from my demons
They're waiting oh so near
Feeding me my memories of everything I fear
Gripping to edges of my soul
In the darkness they drag me down
Waiting for me to sink, waiting for me to drown
With all this weight I desperately hold to
I can no longer swim
There's no air and I can't breath
There's no way I can win
The pain in my chest is excruciating
And I'm shaking to core
There's a warning from my demons
They're waiting for time to give me more

--Shoulder demons

Shoulder demons whisper to my ear
Forked tongues that stab into my very soul
Tortures of the mind and stab at my fears
Speaking its lies and forcing the tears
Steering my thoughts like cattle
One by one to the dark place
I try to see past the veiled lies
Ignore the whispers
But in the distance I see nothing

--Wishes in the Night

Waiting for the end to come
Everyday trying to survive
Waiting for the next
But I can't hold on anymore
I'm tired and worn
Looking for signs
Perhaps the next shooting star will be the one to end it all

--The search

The universe in my mind conspires against me.
My heart sees a hope that my mind can't find
The universe shows a future my minds eye can't see
My soul screams for what others can't hear.
My heart aches for what can't be touched.
Where are you piece of a whole
So close I can taste, smell so near
Like a memory not quite forgotten
Without a map I search
Without sense will I find?
Pulling against my body and soul
The universe conspires against me

--Don't let me disappear

God don't let me disappear
Hold my hand so I know your there
Hold me so I don't float away
In my silence let me know I am heard
Because when I speak I don't feel acknowledged
Let me know, I'm still here
I'm not ready to be a ghost
Free me from myself
God, hold me and don't let me disappear

--Inescapable Gaze

It's hard to find a place to hide
When you're running from what's inside
Distractions in the shadows only go so far
No matter where you go, there you are
Constantly at war with me
I'm my own worst enemy with cuts and scars no one else can see
Bleeding and tired, I don't wanna fight anymore
I can no longer look in the mirror
Behind shallow eyes, dark truths and lies
but I can't escape my own gaze
I am always there, looking out
And I've been like this for days
Denying it for weeks, months, years
So many days, so many ways
How long have I been this way?
How long do I have to stay?
I have lost track of time again
Shatter the glass, break the mirror
Let there be no more smoke
Release this jaded soul
Sweet relief help me
Take me away from me

--Bully in the Mirror

The greatest bully of my heart
I tried so hard to fight back
But you continue to knock me down
The things you tell me
I'll never be good enough
Always alone
Never to be loved
As trials of life leave me worn, battered and bruised
I can't look you in the eyes as you continue to cut down my soul
It's raining again as water falls from the sky
Please not again
Nobody hurts me as much as you do
My own worst enemy
The man in the mirror

--Call Out

I could call out and I know that I should
But my voice has atrophied to the point I don't know if I could
What was once a roar is now less than a squeak
My confidence has become horribly weak
I know I have friends and they say to reach out
But I feel so unheard, even when I shout
My soul screams with everything that I feel
But this life feels so completely and utterly unreal
I don't want to be a bother, I don't want to be a burden
So I shut the door and pull the curtain
I lie here in the empty, the dark
I listen to the lies that the demons remark
What could you do?
What would you change?
You're nothing but stupid, weird and strange
You have no purpose
You'll never be enough
And these voices get louder and louder as life gets more tough
So what can I do, what can I say
My mind is all gone, even when you try to get me to stay
I try to hold on, but is it even worth it
I'm so tired and weak and left without purpose
I feel so alone, even when you're right there
You tell me to talk about it as if you somehow care
But your responses have changed, they're further apart
And so the darkness gets closer and the demons restart
And so my heart feels more broken and I continue to fall apart
Maybe I'm paranoid, maybe it's lies
Maybe I'm the demon who lies in disguise
I look in the mirror. It's all in the eyes.
I'm smiling on the outside, but my soul it still cries.
Please help, I'm cold and alone
And the demon has taken over this once beautiful throne
And so I could try to call out, I know that I should
But this demon is cutthroat, and now I don't think that I could

--This isn't you

Curled on the floor
Alone
I don't want to live anymore
A ghost of me screaming
Get up, this isn't you
Can't you see you haven't lost everything yet
Remember who you are
They're waiting for you to get better
You are loved
Then why do I feel so alone
A ghost of me stands above a shell of what once was
In the hushed darkness, whispers
You can't fix the past, but you still have tomorrow
Get up, this isn't you

--Shadow of a man

Shadow of a man
At home in his prison
Searching for a way out
Dust on his knees for a god that no longer speaks
Voice cracks as he pleads
Devil at his door knocks louder than before
Lost soul hurt and alone
Won't you let me in so I might keep you company

--Purgatory of the Mind

I will rest here with my wicked mind
Resting on a razor's edge
With the weight of my heavy mind with its crushing thoughts
Grinding away at a jaded heart and soul
The edges cutting deep
Do I belong here with these chains I placed upon myself?
The world has become dark
And I can no longer see the way
I guess I will wait out my life sentence
In the Prison of my mind
My life
My purgatory

--Anger burns

Anger burns like hot coals in the throat
You try to scream till the raw emotions leave splinters in your voice
Shackles fresh from the forge hold you to the demons rage
As you face your destruction though glass eyes to be shattered in the minds chaos, how do we touch the world around us
Do you have the strength to release yourself from the hot irons, to let go of what burns us or do you allow the monsters the demons placed inside to consume you
What is the nature of the beast within and do we ever truly have control or just the illusion that we can control our pain.

--In the cold of the Night

In the cold of the night, the demons knock at my window
You had knocked down my walls I put up to protect myself
Easy to let them in
They crawl into my bed now
They ask if we can play
They ask if they can stay
I made them a deal
To weak to fight back, I play with my demons
Tonight I let them win
Another scar upon my heart is the only price I pay
Tonight my demons win

--I'm at a point of no return

I'm at a point of no return
Time to take all of what I learned
My life's turned my heart cold
I've become stern
Because I can no longer morn
As my life takes another form
I know I can't feel this way anymore
Wondering who and what its for
This pain that I keep inside
I wanted to confide in you
But I can't trust no more
So insane I go
Because I hit an all time low
Rock bottoms where I'm at
So tired and weak
So here I sat
I waited beside the road
But nobody came
So I put my dark sunglasses on to hide my shame
In my soul, and I look like a fool
When its cloudy, rainy
All the pain inside you don't even see
You can't judge because, you don't even know me

--Let me go

Maybe it's ok to be drowning
Maybe it's ok to be lost
In the depths of my own heart
Where shadows roam and darkness reigns
If there is no pain
With my last breath
Maybe I could fly
Could you just tell me it's alright to go
Even if you can't see me, I could stay right by your side forever
Look inside you'll find I have to go
Ride or die still ends in death
I am lost and in pain, but
Even in pain I'll still give you my last breath
I love you, so just let me go

--Death my dear old friend

Death oh death my dear old friend
You're always there in the end
No one can run, no one can hide
From your cold the truth, you never lied
You treat the livening all equally
Some day soon they all will see
Death my dear old friend

But I fear you not, you can be kind
When you come for me I won't mind
I have nothing here to leave behind
I have no friends or family
I have no food or money see
So another minute you dare not lend
So my life I let you rend
And so I greet you
Death my dear old friend

--Playing with myself

I play with myself
Emotional abuse
Pain mixed with pleasure
When the pain feels good
I tell myself this will be the last time
But can I know any other way
I play with the highs
Pushed back down by the lows
Verbal foreplay messing with my head
Fingers grasped firmly to my brain
Will I make it through the night?
How long will I last?

--No one understands

Yes, I'm sad, but it doesn't seem to matter
To those I tell deem it just idle chatter
But I'm hurt inside, and I just don't know
How much should I say, how much should I show.
It hurts more to share, when you to seem not to care
And for me to seem not to care seems wrong and unfair
I pray for the answers and pray for some hope
I pray for the time and strength it will take to cope.
Please help me when you see, I just want to feel.
Like somebody cares, someone who's real

--Lonely Wisps

Wisps and shadows
Untouched by the physical world
As indistinguishable voices and whispers pass by
Reaching out to the smoky veil
Screaming out to be held
What do you do when a soul feels alone?
As the hole in my heart grows bigger
As smoky hands reach out only to be blown away
Reach out, don't reach out
The hole grows bigger
I try to hold on to what I am
But how does smoke keep form
Longing to be solid, to be held and heard
When it longs to be intertwined with another
To no longer be alone, but can hold no form
Screaming out from the pain of a missing piece, but given no voice
To hold what isn't physical as it has no form
To dance and be free like the other wisps in the night
Longing to be another light in the dark
What do you do when a soul is lonely?

--I lied

I lie behind jaded eyes
A line behind I say I'm fine
I'm not fine
But do you even care
Fair weather friend
Where are you when cloudy day turns to stormy night
When the rains fall
You come not with umbrella in hand or lantern on darkest night
I am lost in these woods
You are nowhere to be found
I am all alone as I bury my soul
I lie behind jaded eyes
As Foggy days cloud my mind
As I become cold and the world becomes distant
I've reached out before and been swept bye
As subjects change
But these thoughts are to much for one to carry
Let it crush me beneath the weight
I no longer care
I lie behind jaded eyes
Do you even know?
Do you even care?
It's been so long now
I wouldn't believe you if you did.
You say any time
But you never learned the language
You don't know the dialect
I can no longer try explain to those who don't wish to hear
For those with no ear
I will disappear into the fog of myself where you will never find me
And lie behind jaded eyes

I will lie and tell you
I'm fine

--I don't want to care

I don't want to feel, I don't want to care
To leave my heart open to the spring breeze air
Because what if I'm happy?
What if I fall in love?
What if spring brings me a dove?
But happiness always leaves
And falling always hurts
The spring dove brings not a leaf
But it's a crow and it's a curse
What if I opened the door to early or to late?
Winter chill settles in because I miss read the date?
I'm scared of what might come inside this heart if I leave it open
A bitter chill of winter and heart left to be frozen
What if the door is closed and someone finally stops to visit?
Thank you for coming all this way I'm sorry that I missed it
Or what if they went on past to the neighbors down the road?
To run out the door and say I'm here, my heart is not that bold
I'm really scared if you did stop by of what you might think
What if you just walked away? My heart would probably sink
My door would just shrink away to a window, a hole, a wall
So I don't want to feel, I don't want to care at all
I don't want my heart to hurt
Maybe if I pretend it isn't there
Maybe it won't fall, and I'll find you still didn't care

--I don't want to be strong

I no longer want to be strong
I'm tired and sore
Every day I feel like I'm on fire and I'm burning to the core
I'm trying to be strong, but I feel me getting weak
I'm not going crazy it's just been a week, a month, a year I'm just a little unwell
I tell you I'm okay, I'm fine, everything's swell
But I'm not okay
I am not fine
I lie to you and give you a line, so you don't have to act like you're worried this time
Because if you were, I wouldn't feel this way.
Everyday I try and pretend to be okay
But every night is the same replay as I hold myself back from going insane
Alone and secluded sometimes for days on end.
I'm not worth the effort to even pretend
Because when all is said and done
I'll still end up crying alone
Most can't be bothered to pick up a phone

I no longer want to be strong
I am tired and sore
Broken and bruised
I'm not good enough to carry on with life's trials anymore
To make deals with the devils inside my mind for the price of more scars on this heart that is mine
Scars no one can see but me
I feel them deep in my soul
Still burning from the salt falling from cloudy skies to the sea
Constantly burning and tearing back open my heart, only to heal again with holes
Missing pieces of me
How can I ever be good enough when all I am is missing pieces and cracked glass
A once beautiful mosaic, broken from sitting to close to the edge to many times before

If I fall again I might not be able to get back up and reassemble the pieces again
My strength is leaving me
And I'm finding it harder to hold on
And this weight that I carry is just getting heavier.
I want to give up
I'm tired and sore
God please tell me, what is this punishment?
What is it all for?
I'm alone, crying again on the cold hard floor
And how much more am I meant to endure?
I feel I'm not meant to be part of this world
And I don't want to be strong anymore

--To lock away emotion

To lock away emotion
To never feel a thing
Is like caging a canary
And never let it sing
With so much I want to know
So much I want to feel
To lock away emotion
And never break the seal

To choose one emotion
Of that of which to feel
To lock away the others
And never break the seal
But what above the others
Is worthy of the claim
To feel but one emotion
Let it not be felt in vain
Maybe I'll feel love
But in loves rejection, all that's felt is pain
Perhaps I'll go with anger, perhaps I'll go insane
With all the sadness held inside, holding back the strain
All emotion bursting forth, as if it has something to gain
Jealousy and greed, go hand in hand I'm sure
And the feelings lust, of which I should deter
Perhaps I'll go with the will, the power to move on
But then I have to stop and think for hope must be the way
I have so much to hope for, each and every day

--Silent Sirens

In the silence it's so loud
I'm drowning in the ocean as I hear the sirens call
They tell me I'm not good enough, I won't last long, I'll never get what I want if I can't get what I need
I want to reach out, but I don't want to bring you down
I can't tread this water alone forever
Cover my ears, throw me a life preserver
I'm sinking
I can hear the voices screaming
But I can't hear yours
Shield my heart from the waves and tell me I'm not alone

--Pain Killers

Addicted to the pain, but not the pain killers
The ache in my chest
I've relapsed again
And now I swim in the empty emotions
Embracing the feeling of drowning
Synthesized chemistry in my brain
Making me feel so numb

--Minute till Midnight

It's a minute till midnight
And the stars what a sight
My eyes may be cloudy, but I see them alright, just fine
As the world prepares once more to sing auld lang syne
A brand new chapter, a whole new year
Just a few more seconds and it will be here
5..4..3..2..1
Happy New Year everyone
As I look to the sky, a clear cold night
An angel's kiss
A token of change and things to soon missed

It'll be alright, have no fear
a brand new beginning will soon be here
she says as she wipes away a tear
It's been to long this year for you
And now it's time to begin anew
Take my hand it's time to go
As angel wings take time to grow
She takes me away as I disappear
A guardian angel of comforting end
Of broken hearts that might one day mend

--I am not Okay

I am not okay
As I lie here in the purgatory of my own creation
My own hellish isolation
As thoughts scream past and stab at me
My heart, mind and soul
Till the body of the physical world feels every mark
Cold stone of my cell the only comfort
I am not okay
As the floor floods from my eyes
I'm drowning in the sorrow
No hope from tomorrow
I don't want to die, but I have no strength to go on
So I lie here in the dark covered in sad choices and memories
I am not okay
As I hope and I pray of others happiness over my own
Undeserving of the kindness of release.
I ask the judge to sentence me to another day, a month, a year
Fear of unworthiness strikes again
And I return to my isolation
I am not okay
As day after day
I punish myself for everything I have or haven't done.
It should have been more
I should have been better
Yet I hold tight to the scarlet letter.
I love to much, I love to strong
But I feel everything I do is wrong
I feel that I am not okay

--my body weak

My body weak, my heart is cold
I stand aside, watch life unfold
I don't know how, I don't know why
I'm always watching life go bye
Like locked glass doors, how do I get in
I fear life will pass by again
Where do I start, how do I begin
Life's next journey, begin an end

Spring

*Hope, Thoughts
   Connections and Wanderings*

--Healing change

Castles crumble, city's fall
Non are meant to endure it all
Generations change and ruins wither
Kings and Gods one day forgotten
When man's heart no longer beats to the drum
Crushed by the third rock
May it cry the first dew of mourning
As it flows to the stream of time
And once the floods pass
Wash all away with the season
So cold winter turns once more to healing spring

--Winds of Change

What say you winds of change
I hear you, yet I do not understand
I feel you pulse beneath my veins
What do I name you
For you seem not good nor evil
For like the earth and air you are there
I stand beneath you as I watch the world turn
Look there to sky
Blink and you miss it
A burst of light
A shooting ember
And again you whisper in my ear
I feel you all around me
I breathe you in
I close my eyes to the night sky and listen
What say you o winds of change

--Sinking heart

Why is it that I feel so deeply
My love is like an ocean
And I always sink so far the weight becomes crushing
I need someone to catch me in their nets
Bring me to the surface so I can breathe again
Breathe new life in me
Alone it's cold at the bottom
Touch my heart so I know I have not become numb
Take me to the sun so I can feel its warmth
Be the rock I lay my head upon as I rest my soul
And never let me sink beneath my waves of my emotions again

--Crossing Paths

You cross my mind like we once crossed paths
Unexpectedly
As one turns there you are
I look back and wonder, how many times did our paths cross
Pasts intertwined in places unexpected
Were we always meant to meet?
I smile to think we could have met sooner
Despair in knowing there was the possibility we never would
My mind wanders these paths frequently
Always returning to the places where we once met
Thoughts and feelings flooding the path
So I wait and remember
Will we meet again?
Another crossing in time to be frozen in the map of memory
In another life?
You cross my mind often and sometimes it makes me smile
Do I ever cross yours?

--field of flowers

You are a rose in a field of flowers
And I am a bleeding heart

--Hope is

Hope is like moon rays and rain drops
You feel it on your face and on you skin
Let it soak down to you heart and your bones
You feel it in that little place in your soul till the sun comes out again
But only if give yourself the chance to go outside and experience it

--Empty

You don't know the hell I've been though
The price I've paid
To rebuild my soul
I tore everything off the walls
Every bit of me
Floating in the void
I became cold
No one there to hold
I was bracing the walls till I realized I needed to tear them down
To bring in a new me
I had to be empty

--Surgeons Table

I'm not crazy I'm just a little unwell
But I don't need you to place me on a table to dissect me
I don't need you to hold the knife with shaky hands to cut away the parts of me that are hurt and dying
I need you to hold my hand till the fevered dreams go away
Don't try to fix me, because you might slip as I thrash in my delusions, you might slip the knife into an already bleeding heart becoming just another stitch on an already scarred soul
And when you fail to save me like so many have before, don't walk away from my dying body, but please find the strength to stay with me to morn the loss I have for living
Before I slip away, can you hold my hand to the very end
Stay with me and perhaps by some miracle in time I'll heal
Stay with me and with time, maybe my heart will beat again

--Words on a Page

Are we just words on a page?
If not written today forgotten tomorrow
How do we make our mark?
Permanent pen, chisel and stone?
Is a grave our only monument only to be removed in time?
How will we be remembered?
Are our stories predestined, preserved?
If my tome is placed upon a shelf who will pick it up?
Clean off the dust cover
Read it from front to back.
To say in witness I was here?
If I rest upon the shelf, if the story is missing will anyone notice?
If I poured my heart into the pages, what would you see?
Hope and love
Pain and regret
Can hearts forget even if we want to?
How deeply are we intertwined in our own stories?
Are we heros or villains?
Will we have tragedy's or happy endings?
Can I skip to the end?
Would I want to if I could?
What would I have missed?
What have I written so far?
Can you tell me the words on my page?
The ones I can't bring myself to read
Can I read yours?
Has the narrative changed?
And what is left unwritten?
What is the story?
If we were just words on a page

--I Worry about You

You worry about me
Yet you're the one that leaves to many tabs open in my mind
Searches I still have yet to get answers to
of conversations you say we'll come back to
Its complicated… so you say.
Help me find the answers to the questions that answers to more mystery's
I am here with you now searching for the you that is inside
My Iris, would you let your heart bleed to know you're alive?
Just for you my royale, I will break my silence
If I could find the words, break all the rules
Would you still be there?
If I loved you through a periscope
Could my low spirit be good enough
To lift you up
If I held you close, would you close the tabs
Even if the world wouldn't understand, I just wanna know who you are
I worry I might never get the chance

--idk

Hating not the fact that I don't know
What to do or where to go
With this strange new hunger that I feel
Feasting upon the thoughts like it's my last meal
Consumed by feelings that I don't understand
While I wander this new and untraveled land
I'm told I'm fine, but I think "you fool"
I just don't know and that's not cool
Battle raging in my body and mind
Waiting for the truth in the answers I will find

--Days end

A violent past, the suns warm rays
How I long for the days
The happy nights, at summers end
I hope that they come again

--Alone I pray

Alone I pray, like yesterday
for words hope tomorrow
Alone I pray, like every day
for words of strength, not sorrow
Alone today, again I pray
for words of love and wisdom

--closed doors

Behind every closed door is an ear that willing listen and a voice inside waiting to be heard

--Soul fire

Who would I be if I set my soul on fire
Allow my self to scream to the universe
I will not back down
There are days when I feel I don't deserve love
Who would I be if I let myself be happy
Who would I be if the old me was still here
I hold the hand of my angel
Every time I slip they don't let me fall

--Who am I?

I was no longer myself
I didn't know who I was anymore
And in looking in the mirror
I saw it in my own eyes
I was my own demon all along
Behind closed my eyes I knew it was my own voice I heard all these years
I was my own devil
In my fall I needed a search for change
An outcast in my own skin
I need a reason to know
What is it all for?
It's time for a change
This is my redemption

--Oh pillow beneath my head

Oh pillow beneath my head
Every night when I go to bed.
Oh the secrets to you I share
I hold you close and know your there
If you left, oh how I'd cry
So hard it is to say good bye
For all I want is for one to hold
Every night when I get cold
Oh pillow beneath my head
I love you

--Feeling of Nature

The wind through the trees
The rain that falls in the night
Standing on the edge of a mountain
The weight of the world as you look to the sky
Gravity as you fall in an empty field
Floating in the waves of time
Sinking as the world sleeps

--Mad Hatters Well

Beautiful dream
My wonderful rabbit
Late in the timing
I have fallen
To drink from the well
Is to hold from the handle
Of the lost ladle only to realize it's double edged sword
Comfort in the grip of knowing
Sadness in point at my throat
Yet there's hope in the hatter
and comfort in the madness

--A glance in the eye

A glance in the eye
A moment in time
A pause in the moment
A beat with a resounding **stop**
Be still my beating heart
My chest
Relaxed pain
Petrified
Eyes meet as you walk on by
Hopes, dreams, light up like fireworks in the continuum, then fade
After image captured in the mind
Then nothing
What happened?
When the moment was just a dream
I look away
Heart beats again
Breathe

--God I'm Falling

God save me, because I'm falling
And my soul can't afford to be falling in love
I reach for the stars as they're crashing around me
This meteor stuck me in the heart

--Beauty in the fall

There's beauty in the fall
I maybe in pain in the ritual of when 2 hearts meet
Your everything I've ever dreamed of
And even right in front of me I feel the distance between our souls
I believe we are something more
Do you feel it too?

--I want to believe

I want to believe
But I cannot conceive
The truth, when everyone lies

I want to believe
When I grieve
The loss of faith and innocence

I want to believe
When all we weave
Is our thread of lies

I want to believe
When I see
That another loved one that dies

I want to believe
But no longer naive
I no longer believe in anything
But still...
I want to believe

I want to believe
In the good of one and the good of all
The people that come when others fall
To pick them up and raise them high
Instead of using them, then leave them to die
To tell the truth and never lie
That there is still hope and love in the world
As the futures past become unfurled
To have a friend that will never leave
All I want is to believe

I want to believe

--Always the poet, Never the poem

Always the poet never the poem
Tell me your words, I wish to know them
Would you hold me close?
Could you hold my heart near?
Could you tell me the truth without any fear?
When hearts are of longing to be close to one another
Whether it be friend sister or brother
For someone to be of understanding, love and hope
To have that one person that helps you to cope
Through lives toughest moments, harsh realities
A hand to hold as two souls praying please
Show me your heart, show me your truth
Make me a poem, read me your proof
Whisper it in my ear, shout to the sky
I don't want any room left to deny
Love me so tender, love me so true
Make me your poem, with words I never knew

--tired soul

Tired soul who walks alone
You carry your burden
But as you walk to your dark sun
You carry me to your light
So hold close like treasure
And when you're lost look back
Like footprints in the sand
Know you don't walk alone
Let me carry you to the light
So you can shine

--I am a book Unbound

I am a book, a world unbound
A living ruin, left crumbling to the ground
I am a tree, I bloom in the spring
I am Icarus, I flew too high and now I'm falling
I am a lion, king on my throne
I am a wolf, powerful, but alone
We are the stars and the space between
Our souls are the painting that remains to be seen
The sun and the moon they circle and dance
Life is a story of drama, tragedy and romance
A mystery thriller, yet to be solved
A story unfinished, a world evolved
I am a book, a world unbound
So pick me up, read me and find what can be found

--Dream of a lost friend

I was told we couldn't be friends anymore
In the dark, I saw my bleeding heart in my hands
No longer beating, I let it fall to the ground
In the dark you saw its bloom
You whispered if only I knew
If only you reached out
I'd have left a light on
Waking up
Was it just a dream? Or a premonition?
Checking my phone you were still there
The light trying to shine through

--You are my shield

I draw my sword to the fork tongued demon
As it gnashes its teeth
Words whip, thrown like knifes
As my armor slowly falls away
I bare my scars, but my strength is fading fast
Each word a feint, an unavoidable stab at my mind
I'm caught in a shadow of doubt
As I fall, the devil takes one last stab at my mind
And in my moment of need
You shielded my eyes
My ears
And my soul
You became my new armor
My strength
My shield
In that moment I realized
I had forgotten that battles are not won alone

--yearns for the moon

He yearns for the moon
To anchor his heart
Yet in his dreams of looking up forgets that beauty blooms
here on earth

—Calming presence of a faceless angel

Head in lap
Fingers through hair and down back of neck
Eyes closed
As every fiber of muscle and soul relax
No words
But a sense of it's ok
I'm here
And I'm not going anywhere

--Destiny

Haunted by this memory
Over and over repeated I see
Was it a mistake or was it meant to be
I may never know
But may it lead me to where I need to go
Destiny

--Watching her dance

Watching her as she does her dance
Puts my mind into a trance
Scared, afraid, do I take that chance
Take her hand and go for romance
To call it love, that makes me sing
Don't let this be a one time thing
I want her, she's the only one
I love her more than life loves the sun

--It feels like nothing else matters

It feels like nothing matters
If I spoke into the darkness
Could you hear the words I'm saying?
In the distance between us
Can you feel me looking out?
Through time and space
If I screamed would you feel this ache in my heart?
The pain of how much I'm missing you
Echoes throughout my universe felt night and day

What I think
      How I feel

There is nothing I can do or say to change the facts

In my heart
      nothing else matters

--I wish I wish that I could fly

I wish, I wish that I could fly
Way up high into the sky
Flying though the cool breeze air
Living life without a care
Flying high and feeling free
Knowing its a part of me

If I could fly way up high
All the way across the sky
Floating on the cool wind breeze
And over all the stormy seas
Never ever stop to perch
I'd never stop my endless search
The silver lining at rainbows end
A message past I would send
For hope there will always be
For the future you and me

—Hold me like you love me

I just want someone I can wrap my whole soul around and never worry about letting go-
-but I will always worry one day they will leave and eventually I'll have to let go.

--Broken heart of mine

Why do you continue to try, oh heart of mine
Rejected so many times, yet you still persist
Falling for those you can not have or will never love you back
We will never be good enough
I have tried to shoot you down when you attempted to fly away
Yet when I put you in a birds cage, you continue to sing
I have ground you to dust in an apothecary's mortar and pestle
Yet your dust still seeps into my skin and each breath I breathe you in
Infecting me with your fevered dreams that anything is possible
There is still hope
Why?
Why can't I throw you away?
My heart
You are a weight inside my soul
A scar inside my body I can't let go
Trapped in the cage that is my chest
Beating like a drum, a constant reminder that I'm still alive
Don't you know I care, that is why I chain you down and lock you up
I can't ignore this pain you put yourself through any longer.
This cracked porcelain can't hold much more
So please don't break yourself anymore than you already have

--Thoughts in the night

Thoughts, tastes, touch, sound
Waves of memory wash over me like a symphony of sound in the night
Like a melody of music I can barely remember
Dancing in the back of my mind
And when the last note plays
Like a dream, it's over
A moment you can never feel again
But like music, replay forever till the end

--Shooting Stars

If shooting stars granted wishes
I'd pull down all the stars in the sky till it came crashing down on me
Just-
      for a moment of happiness

—Fireworks

I want someone to look at me like that someday
Love and lights
Explosions in the night sky
Glitter and sizzle as they fall over the lake
And after it all
When the light dims
Heart shapes and willows
On the backdrop of our eyes, where there is still the afterglow

--Life's concert

Life's a concert when you open your heart to the tune
Remember to hold tight the melodies
Sing so all your fans can hear
And let the stage lights shine in

--I listen to the music

I listen to the music, the old and the new
It reaches deep inside, with feeling the emotions they ensue
Like the artists can relate the problems I'm going though,
Every time, they hit, the right spot and find the real you
Whether you're happy, look crappy, or just feelin blue
My playlist stuck on shuffle and repeating songs not one time but a few
As I listen to the words, on getting over you
Or maybe shit, in life, just happens; try to get over it and through
There's no point in suffering, punchin a hole in your heart, an pissin a fit
Cuz then you throw your life away, no, you gotta stand up to your fears,
Get up an fight the all tears
And then be strong for as long as you can
Don't look back, at the foot prints laying in the sand
Just let the music carry you, and renew

So then listen to those songs, both the old and the new
The message that they tell, only to the few
And look to yourself; don't put your story on the shelf
That's not the way, cuz I want you to live everyday
Like a happy ending, no, beginning to your life
Its worth living
You'll see soon

--When the music starts

When the music starts
And the bass beat starts, bumpin
I feel it in my heart, heart starts thumpin
An I feel it in my body, I feel it in my soul
That hidden part of me, suddenly made whole
Listen to the lyrics and you suddenly know
What should you do, where to go

Your thoughts and feelings, an artist inspires
Like they take a moment in your mind to re-wire your wires
Setting your soul on fire
Like you can be risen slowly higher
And I love it cuz all it takes is that one song
To explain all the love, the fear and the hate, you've felt all along
And you hear it speaking to you, and you know that its fate
Giving you hope, its not to late
To change for the better

And other people sit and they wonder
Why you dance in the rain and the thunder
Like the spot light is on you and you lighting it up
Like you've just been hit by lightning, but you were thunder struck
And you look them in the eye like you don't even give a f**k
Cuz you know you're finally alive
And that you can survive
And it's absurd how the power hidden in every word
Gives you the strength that was once obscured by only the thoughts of your mind
And then you finally find yourself
Believing again instead of bleeding like when
You were down and out
An all you could do is just scream and shout

But as the beat keeps beatin
And you get out of your seat
You cant help it, as your moving your feet

And that tune is hard to beat, as you go into heat

And all it takes is that song
The one that's been with you all along
To help you to never give up that fight
To make sure that you're always doing alright
To get you though the day and then though the night
Cuz when you're a star, you'll shine so bright
And your light will take you far

--I feel a change

All around me I feel it
Like a spike in my brain
An ache in my bones
As I attempt to remove the weight I've carried for so long
There's a change coming
What will time bring
What will I become
The gentle giant in my soul dressed for battle for so long

--shining eyes

Hiding behind shining eyes
You spend your life waiting to show your love
Joy in the moments near
Sadness when far
Run to me
Follow where I go
Keep close and never leave
With love that will never fade.

--Random thoughts

My mind expands and then contracts
I turn my head and face the facts
My train of thought, I trace the tracks
I ponder, water, the flood of memories
Wonder, wander, not all thoughts lost
Forgotten, found in lands unbound
The random, the mad, insane, afraid
The universes that we made

--Removal of thoughts and sound

Silence
Like drops of water in ripples of space and time
Each drip drop forming gentle waves
Washing over like a relaxing heartbeat
Peace from chaotic noise of the other world
With each drip drop
Weight lifted
Lighter than air
Drift away
Freedom in the void
Relaxation in the nothingness
All alarms subside and I reset
And bask in the warm glow of the sun

--I meditate

I meditate, I calm my mind
All the thoughts inside I find
I build them up, I let them flow
I step way back and then I know
Emotions I feel, get in the way
I try to hold them back at bay
I make them stop and then I say
I reclaim my mind today

--Inspiration in the night

From slumber the inspired mind wake
As brightness blinds the tired eye
Cannot wait till morning
No
Lest the inspiration fade like a waking dream
Write now the words before they ebb into the ether
And when read again in the waking hours
You'll thank me in the morning
Sincerely
Inspiration in the night

--Moon rises with beautiful melodies

Moon rises with beautiful melodies that
Wax and wane in the air of the night
Like a breeze sending shivers down my spine, but who's soft touch warms my bones
Between each silencing note tremors before beams of light as the stars conduct their symphonies. I stand before the conductor as I watch the masterpiece untold.
Till with warm glow of the sun rises in rainbows of color and the world weeps with morning dew. The world turns once more to the sights and sound, then once more the sun sets in brilliant glow prepares for act two.
And the Moon rises with beautiful melodies.

--I have an art

I have an art I cannot express
In my heart an explosion of colors
Painted on the winds with a splattering of swirls like a Van Gogh
Each sound a symphony orchestrated to the beat no note can hit and no ear can describe
My body can't trace the lines my minds eye can see
No brush can match the strokes of beauty my heart can feel
No words can define the meaning
And no language can translate to the picture of a thousand words etched on my very soul
Not even the finest marble could be chiseled to its likeness
If I could, I would show you the vibrant colors no eye can see and no rainbow can produce
On a canvas, so large, no frame can contain it
So grand, no mind can conceive it
Art so emotional, no feeling can express
In the beauty of nature we all have an art we cannot express

--Flood of you

How do I survive the flood of thoughts of you, when waves of you crash into the valleys of my mind.
My ark might not have been built survive the highs and lows.
No winds for my sails, but these waters cast me to toss and turn.
Where is my dove?
I hold on tight, but for what?
How many nights and days will I last on these waters till I see the land of hopes and dreams.

--Poetry in your hair

You have poetry in your hair
Stars in your eyes
A smile that outshines the sun and moon
Angels in your voice
Heart in your soul

--glass boats

2 souls
Glass boats on the waves
Yet we dare not reach out
For to be close risk shattering the hull
I admire your beauty from afar
May life's cruel waves never chip your glittering ship
To glittering shards of glass

--My forever missed

Forever young, forever missed
A scar left on my heart like a gentle kiss
Gone to soon, a lesson learned
Life goes on, some days burn
As rain falls on a tempered soul
I yearn to go back to days of old
To be held by you, shielded from the blaze
You saved me from life's darkest days
Hand on shoulder you guide me out
Shining, you light the way
Always hope that makes me stay
My scar on my heart, my forever missed

--To my mother

I'm sorry if I didn't turn out the way you wanted.
I'm sorry you weren't here to see how I turned out
I'm sorry you weren't here
I hope in the next life
I can fill your heart with stories of all my adventures
I hope in the next life I can give you the strength to stay

--Dark gardens

Flowers still bloom in the dark garden
A kaleidoscope of colors of mixed slate black and grey
As we bury the sunlight
The moon still peaks bright behind thick clouds
In the dark wood of a lost world
Thick dew drops from the rose to the pond below
As a dark rainbow arches across the sky

--If you were a flower

I wish I could pluck you up and take you home
But what right do I have to take you from yours
Your beauty shines in the sun from the fields around you
To move you from your soil will you still grow?
Can I provide the nutrients for your soul?
I want us to grow together
Intertwined and rise up, summer into fall to winter
Then again in our next lives of spring

--Masked illusions

How is it that this world is so full of magic. Yet so few can see it. Masked by illusions, confusions, delusions. Walls built by our own deceptions to keep ourselves safe in false hopes that the world outside isn't as cruel as inside our minds. But if we could just climb above that wall and see from the greater view, the greater magics hidden from us, perhaps one day we could glimpse the magic of life, love and understanding of the grimoire of life.

--Refractions

I could no longer see the light at the end of the tunnel
I bent myself till I nearly broke
In the absence of light
The dark swallowed me whole
I was feeling heavy as I was drowning in myself
I was lost and I couldn't find myself
Deprived of my voice
I could only hear the echoes that weren't me
I was being buried alive
Holding onto the walls trying to find my soul
Where is the light within?
If only I'd open my eyes
I'd see the light that had already shown through

--Waiting

Talking to the sky
Empty rooms and walls
Why does The Universe give only
Blank signs and empty promises
Why does my heart fall upon deaf ears
Seen only by clouded eyes
Where is the hope I was told was so near
The change that is so close
I lie here and whisper
I'm here and I'm still waiting

--Wanna hear my deal I made with God?

Do you wanna hear the deal I made with god?
That if only we could be happy
I would give up anything
Would my life be good enough?
Can you survive without me?
Will the world still move on?
How would I know that it was all worth it?
What lies in the dark?
Could I battle all our demons if I had god on my side?
Battling a holy war inside ourselves if I was a ghost
Do you wanna hear the deal I made with god?

--I'm Sorry My Friend

I'm sorry my friend, I hope this finds you well
This poem is for you, I hope that you can tell
Since the day we met you quickly became my best friend
my instant ride or die, till the very end
We spoke all the time and every single day
Talk or text just to be sure we were both okay.
We could talk about anything, rain or shine.
But I'm afraid I may have finally, gone and crossed a line
I could tell you anything, but maybe this time I shouldn't have
I have nothing, but shame
It's not your fault when I'm the one to blame
I should have kept it to myself
to put the thoughts away, labeled do not remove from shelf
I know you say you're fine
But I know it's probably on you mind
I failed you my friend and now I have this fear
That maybe I should just go away, to go and disappear.
I've complicated everything and we haven't spoken all day
I know we've both been fighting demons and both have much to say.
I just want you to know, I miss you and hope that you're okay
No matter what happens and if I have to disappear, just remember you are still the best part of my life and the best part of my year
I'll never understand what you saw in me
You cared and I don't know why
But you are still my best friend, my one and only ride or die
I'm sorry

--Curse of a Bleeding Heart

Curse of a bleeding heart
To feel everything all the time so intensely
If you only knew how close to the edge I am
I'd still sacrifice my beating heart before I lose you

--Trying to seal up my heart

I'm trying to seal up my heart
To wrap it up and place it in a tomb.
But for every brick I lay
You keep knocking down every wall
You seem to find every crack in my heart and make your way in. To wrap yourself around my soul.
Bringing me oxygen
Protecting me from myself.
Lifting the weight I place upon myself so crushing.
To push you away would be impossible because like a magnet the closer you get, the more I'm pulled in.
I cannot hide myself from you
You take every word and feeling with love and understanding, despite circumstance
And the more I try to deny these feelings the stronger they get.
I'm trying to seal up this bleeding heart, but it's bleeding like never before.

--Run and be free

Run and be free
Fly to the sun
And pay no mind the voices
Less they leaden your heart
Remember only angels may touch the stars
So sweeten the dream
Hold your head high
And reach forward

--Poems on my Mind

poems on my mind
words on my lips
like a sweet and gentle kiss

--I love Poetry

I love poetry
The words on the page
The rhythm and rhymes
The wisdom of sage
Written by young or by old
Doesn't matter the age
Read by the mind
Released from the cage
There's freedom in the words
And heart in the chords
Formed in the fires
And tempered in the forge
Poetry speaks, it moves and it flows
Wonderfully tragic emotions that enter our hearts and souls
With words all around us like magic in nature
And it all starts with words just written on paper

--Raw Soul Honest and True

Raw soul, so honest and true
Show me the deepest and darkest parts of you
Hold on to hope, hold on to love
Remember the leaf brought by the dove
Let go of the sadness, let go of the past
Remember life will sometimes move on to fast
Don't let this world change who you are
Remember your journey and keep raising the bar
All of the highs and all of the lows
The struggle up hill that nobody knows
You are worthy and strong, you are enough
The things that we go through, life will get rough
The weight of the 3rd rock, the heaviest stone
Was never meant to be carried alone
Others are here, so try to reach out
Even when your mind is flooded with doubt
There is a light in the dark and it travels far
So look to the moon and look to the stars
There are cracks in your heart that let the light in
So let it be your guide, beginning to fin

--Shadow of Hope

Dark places beneath cloudy sky's
As I still know the moon shines bright above
And the stars yet glow
May the winds soon shift
That you might look up to see
That sliver of light

Summer

Love, Friendship,
*　　　　Happiness*

--from beneath the mulberry tree

Old memories beneath the summer sun wash over me as I stare deep into the sea of your eyes
Under the mulberry tree I could have laid with you forever;
What could have been, maybe
Every long goodbye with you in my arms my soul cried out to kiss you
I never knew if you shared the feeling,
and in my doubt
I let you slip away
but in my memory, I'm not moving from beneath the mulberry tree
J, forever in my heart

--a midsummer daydream

Hair down
Head on my chest
Laying on an old couch
Window open to the summer sun
This is where my heart wants to be
As it beats in rhythm to yours
A quiet symphony that fills my soul
Cool breeze, I hold you closer
Else the wish blow away like candle flame
Perhaps one day, it will come true.
Laying on an old couch
Just holding you

--calmed, relaxed

Calmed, relaxed
As time does pass
I might finally go to sleep
Get up, go home she says
But I don't want to leave
Let me stay a little longer
So I don't have to let you go

--Love

Love
Two lips like flowers grown close together
Breathing in fresh air
Freely given, but taken away
Bare skin pressed close and warm
Shivers down the spine giving goose flesh
As two hearts beat as one

--Eyes

Eyes
The windows of the soul
Heart
One of two that makes you whole
Hands
Of yours I wish to hold
Lips
That I would kiss
You
Without, I'd surely miss

--Kissing you

The thought of one day kissing you
Sends shivers down my spine
Of holding you close to me
And telling you, you are mine
I love you much, but don't ask why
The reasons are as vast as stars in the sky
I'll hold you closer, I won't let go
I love you more than you will know

--Comforting kiss of fires flame

Comforting kiss of fires flame
Wild spirits that make my soul tame
I sit and watch as you do your dance
Drawing my mind into a trance
Natures art, wild and true
Red flame, yellow flame, blue flame too
With beauty and warmth that brings me closer
Dangerous to all given over exposure

--Beauty of the night fire

Beauty of the night sky
Or beauty of the flame
Both blind me before the other
I want nothing more than to stare deeply into both
To look from the flame to the sky I cannot see the stars
Far and distant like a dream to take me away
A drift in the vastness of the universe
To look from the sky to the flame
The stars twinkle and dance above while I look to the pit below
Do I look away from the flame
Dangerous and close before me
I feel its heat
I am cautious, but close as the wind blows it asks to cuddle against my skin
Like a lover who wants nothing more than to dance
I see the beauty in both the near and far
Beauty I dare not touch

For the flame is close and wants nothing more than to hold me closer and dance as it drys away my tears
And the stars so far want nothing more than to grant my wish to take me away from it all
And all I hear is silence
As I am alone
So I stay where I am
Stunned by the beauty both near and far
A beauty I dare not touch

As the stars and the flame dim into the night, the embers hot
The moon the only one that promises nothing more than to come back once again.

--Sparks of love

To love
To love not lust, because love need not be sexual
To love and hold close another soul like a candle from the wind protected by your space.
To love and build the flame from a spark to a bonfire
Love is fire that burns bright and yet still can hold close and not be burned.
Our souls like suns and stars vast in the sky.
Look up
Let each souls light shine on you that you might spark another.

--Hidden Battles

I'm spinning in my head
I'll tell you I'm fine
Because I have to believe it is true
Hidden battles of which I wish you knew
My heart is beating, telling me I'm still alive
But I'm dazed and confused as I try to survive
My eyes are blind
I cannot see what I'm trying to find
I hear your voice, it's far away
As you hold my hand, begging me to stay
I shake my head, get back in the moment
You kiss my lips
I breathe in air like fine sips
Your hand on chest and a questioning glance
I'm okay
I'm okay
I tell you I'm fine
Because I have to believe it's true

--Let our demons play

It's not far all the things you make me say
Yet you won't let our demons play
Claws and teeth, dancing the night away
Fur and scales in a beautiful embrace
While a mirror alone we may not be able to face
Each others demons we may chase;
Away with them and let them play
And stand together may we stay
Hold my hand and let's walk away
Hopelessness of skin and bone
Our spirits shall ever rome
But together may we never fall apart
Hold tight to the thread sister spirit
Let the demons play then lay to bed
Satisfied and fed
With lullaby's that make even the angels cry

--How can I know

How can I know something if you don't tell me.
How can I learn if you don't teach me.
How can I love if you don't love me.
I can be an open book, so open me up, write inside
Show me the way
Move and I will move with you
Stay and I will stay with you

--I crave your presence

I crave your presence
Long for your warmth
To hold you close
And kiss your lips
To share my life
And stay with you

—Funerals for the living

We walk with the thoughts and the prayers
Staggering through the emotions
And eventually bury the memory
Seeds of missing you in our hearts
That bloom at the strangest of times
Till we too turn to rest in the dust
You cannot hear our cries as we water your soil
You cannot see the message on the stone
These are for us
The living dead
The temporary
But in us, you are timeless and live on forever

--Ghost of you

A ghost of you still lingers
Like haunting memories I'll never exorcise from my mind
I try to hold you close, but the hands of my mind slip right through
I try to look through the veil as the winds of time blow the image of you away
The tears of time that flow etch away at the memories of your voice
And if you only die twice I'll kneel at your grave and cry your name forever
So your spirit will never leave me
But you will always be missed

--Bury me beneath my garden

Bury me beneath the flowers of my garden that I too might someday bloom
Bury me so that I might still feel the rain and look to the sky as it washes away the tears
     As it falls watch as time erodes away the rocks I laid around my heart
Let stand the tree that I might hear the whispers of the wind
Please visit my stone that I might have company.
Please visit my garden often that I might never feel alone

--Depression in the mind

Like a weed growing in the summer sun
No matter how you pull in the opposite direction
It keeps hold
Roots running deep and spreading far
With every regrowth, comes back faster and stronger than the last
Like a hydra monstrously overshadowing the world
Don't let it control the peace of the garden
Recenter and find the sun

--The Soldier

As I sat there,
In the middle of the field
I lifted my hand from my chest:
Death flowing forth.
The resounding boom still ringing in my ear
I wandered the corridors of my mind.
I found everyone sitting down to dinner,
Their heads bowed over the delicious food.
Farther down the hall I found wife and child,
The child's eyes closed in slumber,
Mother rocking him back and forth.
Farther back still I found a man on one knee,
The woman in front of him crying
Tears of happiness.
Coming back I cried
Unmoving I lay there till
My body turned to the ground.

--The Wanderer

I wonder around the world, to see what I may find
Constricted not by my body, but only by my mind
I wonder around the galaxy, all the planets are still there
I wonder around the universe, all the stars they don't care
All of life that is wondering, what secrets it might share
The universes wonders, so beautiful that I stare
Wonder about in the night, the thoughts that lay within my mind
Enlighten me oh wonders, I wish to know it all
Before the day that I die, the day I'll surely fall

Down in the woods, a tree branch I did trip
Down to earth I tumble, To the ground I hit
Split the earth in two and farther did I fall
Down to hell I went the flames that I saw
Into the belly of the beast and past the monsters maw

Inside the blackened mess, in the dark cauldron did I find
To my surprise a wolf who's teeth glimmered and shined
And then arose two weapons sprung forth from his mind
A sword and shield are all that I could find
Choose the only one I could for they were placed far apart
I chose the shield and not the sword
For I could not kill in sport
It looked at me in confusion, the wolf, when I started to walk away
He followed me as my companion
Forever with me he would stay
Forever in the dark, my friend

Many adventures did we have together
Wondering through this cave
Just me and my wolf, he must be very brave
For trusting in a human wanderer, who kind of needed to shave
They wondered through that cavern
Not knowing if it was day or night
Occasionally being attacked by bandits, who put up a fight

And then one day they reached the end, the end they found the light

Continuing through their journey the wanderer and his friend
Until one day the wanderer, had met his very end
Many years did they travel together through the thick and thin
Not ever knowing the dangers that had always lied within
The full moon glow, the wolf was sad, so howled he did
And every moon after so the lone wolf howled till he went to bed
His friend had been enlightened to a higher plane did he ascend
And soon the wolf had died too
As all wanderers eventually do
We wonder about the universe our angels by our side
Although we may not always see them, our wolfs as they have cried
Will always be there for us
In the wanderers dream

--Feelings you may never know

How do I speak, when I can't find my voice.
How do I see, when I drown in your eyes
How do I think, with the rhythmic pounding of my heart
How do I move, with the paralytic shaking of my body
How do I feel, with the intensity of a soul
My mind melts at the sight of you
Your smile a portrait of perfection
I am both lost and found in your presence
I think I like you and you may never know.

--First thought, last thought

First thought, last thought
I think of you
Night and day
I want to be with you
And forever stay
Take me, claim me
As your own
As long as your with me
Together, I feel at home

--My Friend

She hides golden hair beneath a black veil and dark braids
Blue eyes behind reflected shades
But nothing can hide the smile that out shines the sun
She is the kindest, most caring friend to everyone
A comforting presence that makes the world feel safe
A balance of patience, love and grace
But rain clouds smear mascara lines
She tells the world that she'll be fine
I hold her close, a hug with hearts so near
Life can be so unkind and unclear, but have no fear
I will stay
Until we wipe the final tear away

Beautiful soul, few will know
Please carry your heart and hope wherever you go
I take comfort in knowing who you are
A soul so rare, a radiant star
I hope someday I can help you see
The beautiful person I know you to be

In the crowd, the band plays her favorite song
I hope to hear her sing along
A voice so few will get to hear
But I am close and I hear it clear

She holds my hand, please don't let go
A sign she holds so that I know
I'm not alone in this crowd
My heart skips, is that aloud?
Even in words unspoken, the magic of a silent token
She's saying I am here, don't you forget
A reminder to live and not regret

These words, this page will never be enough I fear
To describe the things, the way, in how I see her
I want to say so much more
I'd pour my heart out, empty the core
To describe the person that I see

And everything she means to me

My best of friends I love the most, I raise a glass, my only toast
I hope that you always try to remember January into December
I am here, don't you forget
I will never have any regrets
The day we met means the world to me
To the nines our bond will March through laughter and tears, my ride or die, I've got your back for years

So beautiful soul, that try's to hide
Behind black veil and shaded eye
Please, please don't try to hide from me
In truth, because I want the world and you to see
The shining star in the silent night that comforts friends and me
And makes life so much better and feel alright

--Blue eyes

Blue eyes
Iris and soul
Cross to touch
What I wouldn't give for a moment.
Hard to breathe when you're drowning
Heart beats hard without oxygen

--Dear Ocean eyes

What treasures do you hide in the depths and shallows of your soul
You look within and see only shadows beneath the waves
But I see stars reflected from the surface within
Galaxies of wonder, so as time flows in you
Never let your rivers flow turn you brackish

--What is Happiness?

What is happiness to me
Happiness is hand holding hand as we're walking down the street
Someone across the dinner table as we accidentally bump feet
Happiness is laying in the grass as we attempt to look at stars on a moon lit night
A hug so tight that it last for hours after
Long talks filled with both tears and laughter
Happiness is time spent with a friend, open talks and feelings and no need to hide or pretend
Happiness is knowing no matter what you'll always be my friend
Happiness is a song that we listen to and can both relate
Another soul to vibe with and completely resonate
Happiness is me knowing you are here with me, knowing that it's the true me you can see
Happiness is butterflies from a midnight kiss
Knowing it's me you truly missed
Happiness is the moment you know you just made a good memory
The excitement of the message or letter you just sent to me
I know they say not to place your happiness on others
But to me happiness is togetherness
Happiness is you and me

--Hazel eyes

I look to her hazel eyes
Like drowning pools
I've fallen in
Lost in a maze between the iris and soul
I steal a glance
Her chest moves with each breath
To touch her angel skin with skin
Lips with lips
From which each word I could hold onto like shelter from a storm
Chest burns from a still heart
Air taken from the lungs
What I wouldn't give for just a moment to hold her hands in mine
But not meant to be, but fantasy

--Pictures

They say a picture is worth a thousand words
But filtered photos are fake currency for the eyes
As nothing can replace the beauty of the real thing
The natural glow of your skin, the breeze through your hair
The sensation of your scent, the feel of your presence, the sound of your breath
You could be as still as the picture
In your presence, the moment, this memory is worth a thousand thousand more words

--Forget the world

Forget the world
Stay with me
Under the stars
Or shady tree
We'll hold hands
And walk together
Just you and me
Two birds of a feather

--If I could tell you everything

If I could tell you everything
I would give you my world
Put it in a book for you to read at your leisure as it explodes
from my mind with tidal forces across the universe
If I could tell you everything
I'd tell you how much I miss you
Another missed shot to connect ends as an arrow in my heart
If I could tell you everything
I'd tell you of the pain I feel inside
Instead, I'll tell you, I'm fine
If I could tell you everything
I'd tell you how much **I love you**
Instead, I'll just stay silent

--My bleeding heart

If I offered you my bleeding heart
Would you walk away in disgust or plant it gently in the ground

If I showed you my tears
Would you dump them down the drain or gather them carefully to water your garden

If you saw my restless soul
Would you run in fear or would you lay it to rest

If you saw me
Would you stab out my bleeding heart or hold my hand and watch the
      flowers
           Bloom

--Just me and you

Just me and you
Nothing to do
But to me that's ok
Just as long as I'm with you
Then happily I will stay

--Hearts bleeding again

Calm as a fall breeze
You washed over me
With simple words you almost made me a believer
Blissful peace expanding like galaxy's over me
Silent as the night
My heart attacked
Bleeding again
Even if she fell in love
You can never hold her in your arms
So sink me again beneath the waves
Wash me away from how I feel
Kill my fear
Only to bring me back again
To show me the way

--Touching Eternity

For a moment in time I touched eternity. With grace in your eyes, I held the world and the stars shown brighter than ever before. But even the sun was eclipsed when our two souls collided.
In a moment-
      everything was known   the world froze
the universe was balanced and nothing else mattered

And after it all-
      after the moment passed-
            after eternity.
                I realized
Forever doesn't last long enough.

--The calm before my storm

You are the calm before my storm
As my mind's like a raging tantrum
You stand before it and ease it to sleep
You hold me like no other
Close, like lightning to thunder
You make me peaceful
The night air, after a light rain
You're like no other
You are the calm before my storm

--Loves battlefield

Heart beats hard to the sound of war drums
Blood burns in my veins like hot fire from the bellows beneath the skin
Muscles ache from the forced march of my heart
I have lost my shield and know not if my soul will survive
Plunge not your sword into my soul, for I only seek the peace from your lips
The drums still beat
How will my soul survive?

--Loves sacrifice

In this modern age we still have human sacrifices
We sacrifice ourselves for the ones we love
No bodies on the altar
But minds and souls
We sacrifice our own happiness for the ones we love on the altars of our minds
That they *might* be happy

--scared, afraid

Scared, afraid of what you might think
I know sometimes I act like such a dink, a dork
You know how I am
A slowly aging childish man
But I want you to know how much I care
For you I will always be there

I'll be there when you need a friend
I'll want to be with you to the end
I love you, I know it's true
But I have no clue on what to do
Lost, confused with these emotions
All these thoughts, causing loud commotions

If you except me for who I am
How could I be the perfect man
For I have never loved like this before
And never will forevermore
No one else could ever make me feel this way
I dream about you both night and day

So please oh please tell me how you feel
And tell me that these dreams, these feelings are real

--Good night

Good night to one,
Good night to all
Tonight I hear the sandman's call
To my bed I once more fall
For the day was long
So much I saw
So tired I am, I'll have to crawl
Like a child I shall slumber
Sawing logs and chopping lumber
So as I try to go to sleep
I'll lay here counting sheep
And once more to you, I say good night
And don't let the bed bugs bite

--Trance

Night and day, I think of you
And I know not what to do
To tell you how I truly feel
Or stay real quiet, alone, an learn to deal
With all the thoughts within my head
They make me happy, then fill with dread
For I know not how you feel
About making fate between us real
For no words can explain, how I feel with you
I wish our hearts to be one not two
Without you, my hearts in pain
Thoughts of you drive me insane
I'm angered at myself in fact
Of confusion on how I should act
For as a friend I confide in you
My thoughts and feelings you left askew
I know not how, I know not why
I wait and think as time goes bye
To show you how I feel for you
I wish, I wish you only knew
My friend, my friend forever more,
I never felt this way before
My heart is open, walk through the door
I think I love you that much I'm sure

--Universe of love

Universes, Vast and far
Are we but passing stars
Shooting across to sky
Longing to be pulled in by gravity
Fear in falling to hard
Burning in the atmosphere
Will there be anything left
Will we fly again
Love brighter than the sun
May it never fade with distance
Or darkest of the nights
We are all moons in our phases
Stars in the night
Planets brimming with life
Galaxy's endlessly drifting
In hopes to one day collide
In the scope of our narrow vision
A big bang as love and life are created once more
May love last longer than the paths we follow
And may we forgive never forget ever we drift away

--My crazy family

My family might be crazy and I might be insane
But I love you all equally, I love you all the same
To all of my friends out there, this includes you
If I didn't have you in my life, I don't know what I'd do
Through the good times and the bad, you always stood beside me
Even though I'm annoying and sometimes very whiny
If anyone ever hurt you, I'd rip them limb from limb
I'd tie them to a rock and make them sink or swim
I might not say it, but you know that it's true
You know that I love you, you crazy persons you

--A bronzed god

Sweat coming from every pore
On a hot summers day
Muscles toned, glisten in the light
Feet black from a hard days dirt
As I change the land
I look to the sun, a bronzed god

--To my friend

Thank for everything you ever did. For protecting me and my heart
You were there from the start
Shield in hand
You lifted me above the crowd
With out you I'd be lost
Hold me close and don't let me go
As long as you hold my hand I know I'll never disappear again

--To the one I love

To the one I love, where ever you may roam
You're always welcome to my home
Any day, anytime
Just sit with me
I'll write you a poem, recite a rhyme
To make you happy, I'll make you smile
Even if it's only for a little while
If your sad I'll hold you close
If you cry I will be here to wipe away the tears
I'll protect you from all your fears
Just for you, I'm always here
For the one I love

-- In the stardust together

If we could be we would be
And not even the stars in the sky could separate us
They would guide us closer till the dust in our veins mingled together for eternity
I would taste you on my lips
Feel you not just in my arms, but in my soul
Entangled like the roots of the world tree touches all the realms
Yours and mine
We could have nothing and yet we would have everything
And in the stardust we could be anything
In the stardust we are everything
In the stardust we're together

--Beautiful Little one

Beautiful little one new to the world
With eyes like little stars
Let me show you the world that you might one day know all it's wonders
Little one with ears so small let me whisper sweet stories
Telling tales of many lives that you might live a thousand of them
Little one with hands so small may all your goals be within reach
No mountain to high no road to long, but always close to home.
Little one with feet so small may you never have to wander
That you might want for nothing and all paths lead you home.
Little one so full of life may all you meet protect you

--Tomorrow

To my Best Friend,
Thank you
Thank you for showing me your world with music
Your patients with my overthinking mind
Your reminders, the promises, the thousand messages that you're not going anywhere
And when I can't hear you words over the screams of my mind
Thank you for shouting just a little louder.
Thank you for not letting me feel alone
I'm sorry for all my doubts and the lifelessness I feel in my soul
Your faith in my future brings light to my world
Thank you for telling me about Tomorrow

--I think I love you

Heart on the floor
And instead of calling for help I called you
My last words
Of all the things I wished to say
Five words come to mind
Waking up
It was just a dream
Is it wrong to want to know if you feel the same?
But in the art of not dying
I'm to afraid of asking for fear of ruining everything
So in my silence I'll say
I'm sorry, Please forgive me

--Even if she falls

Calm
Calm before the chaos of my mind
With a few simple words you brought me peace
With a simple touch you slept
And it was in that peace I finally knew
Even if she falls
Oh heart, why do you do this again?
Wanting what you can't hold
But what is one more crack in the glass

--To the future one

Please be gentle and patient
My soul is fragile and old
The glass is cracked, the porcelain is chipped
The soul is pouring out, but light is shining in
Damage has been done, but maybe you can help pick up the pieces
See the beauty in the art
The flowers of my garden are withered and dry
And there are days when the weeds take over
But tend it carefully, water it each day
Pull each weed before it runs too deep
Handle my soul with love care and patience
Listen to my whispers in the breeze
And even in my silence you'll know how to care for me
Protect me from myself
Help me grow strong again and I too will be your shield.
If I can't see you, reassure me that you are still there.
Never leave my mind to wander, for my soul will get lost in the nothingness. And I don't want to disappear again.
Strengthen my soul with stardust and moonlight and watch with happiness how much our gardens bloom

About the author and poetry

The 4 Seasons
As I reflect on my poetry journey, I'm reminded that emotions are like seasons and while everyone experiences emotions differently The ups and downs, cycles. Many emotions can be mixed and intertwined. And while each season has its own emotions to experience. You can still experience winter in spring and summer in fall. Emotions aren't always linear. They mix and intertwine at times. So while in our seasons we can experience feelings of being alone and loss there is still hope. While we can experience anger and depression there is still love. And as we go though these emotions there is still time to experience the silliness in-between.

Looking back on these poems, I am filled with shock and awe with everything that I've been though. Not truly realizing how I felt until I looked back. Writing these poems was an outlet for a lot of the bottled up emotions I was feeling inside and I never originally intended to share such private and raw emotions. They just come spilling out and writing just came naturally.

There are a few poems that I did share with friends and when I did it resonated with others on a level I didn't know they could. And when it became a collection, it became clear to them (not to me because I had my doubts) that it should be published. That others might resonate too. It's my hope now that maybe it does. Maybe someone else won't feel so alone with their bleeding hearts. Life is hard sometimes, but it doesn't need to be alone.

As I look back and fix <u>many</u> grammatical errors (there are more than I'm proud to admit). I'm in the midst of another cycle- winter. And I am still finding it difficult to reach out. It helps to realize that I have been through this before albeit different circumstances. Difference being I now have the support of friends that are really trying to be there for me. And to them I hope that I am there for you as much as you have been for me.

To anyone struggling with their own bleeding hearts, I offer these poems as a reminder it might feel like you're drowning, but you're not alone. Life is hard sometimes, but it doesn't need to be solitary. This collection is a testament to the power of shared experiences and the human spirit's capacity for resilience. If my words can help, even in small ways, then I'm hopeful that this collection will resonate with others.

Index

Fall

9) The puzzle of heartbreak
10) Your opinion
11) Don't go
12) Eclipse of the heart
13) Be still my heart
14) The seed I'll never know
15) Broken Futures in the Multiverse of Madness
16) My life is crashing down around me
17) On this post
18) Shadows in my eye
19) Ghost of missing you
20) Parting Memories
21) I lost my way
22) If I could tell you Everything
23) Scream to the wind
24) What if it was Me
25) Another day Alone
26) Why is it I feel this way
27) I don't understand
28) Holding back Love
29) Spring
30) So long
31) Iron maiden of the heart
32) I sit here in this empty room
33) life inside this empty room
34) Prison house
35) Reverberations of silence
36) Bad dreams and nightscapes
37) Restless sleep
38) Instability
39) No rest for the Wicked
40) Satellite
41) Melancholy sadness
42) I thought that I was over you

43) Whispers
44) Ever since
45) Surrounded and alone
46) I try to hide
47) Shield Sister
48) Fighting demons inside my head
49) Breaking and Broken
50) Insanity
51) paranoid
52) Emotions rise emotions fall
53) Broken heart, weight of mortality
54) Innocence of Icarus
55) I'm afraid I'll always be alone
56) The wolf
57) Fade away
58) hallow home
59) Now What

Winter

63) What is anger
64) Who am I mad at
65) Isolation
66) Let it be known
67) comfortable floor
68) Tears on the pillow
69) Another day
70) Decoration friend
71) Broken futures
72) My New December
73) World of Negativity
74) Overthinker
75) Wasted time
76) This useless feeling
77) Will I ever be able to sleep
78) Starving love
79) Falling heart
80) Remove my heart
81) I like my mind wander

82) I bow to fate
83) Broken Vacuum
84) G.r.i.n.d
85) Feelings of Jealousy and greed
86) Silent screams
87) Creature of Habit
88) Loud thoughts
89) Picking up the pieces
90) Who was there
91) I want to disappear
92) My friends say
93) I don't want to be alone
94) Gaze of your eyes
95) Don't open, dead inside
96) Wake me up
97) I'm okay
98) Killing heart
99) Missing
100) It will take time to get over you
101) Destructive nature
102) Stained Glass Heart
103) Glass windows of the soul
104) What if
105) I have a Dark Feeling
106) A Warning from My Demons
107) Shoulder demons
108) Wishes in the Night
109) The search
110) Don't let me disappear
111) Inescapable Gaze
112) Bully in the Mirror
113) Call Out
114) This isn't you
115) Shadow of a man
116) Purgatory of the Mind
117) Anger burns
118) In the cold of the Night
119) I'm at a point of no return
120) Let me go
121) Death my dear old friend

122) I play with myself
123) No one understands
124) Lonely Wisp
125) I lied
126) I don't want to care
127) I don't want to be strong
129) To lock away emotion
130) Silent Sirens
131) Pain Killers
132) Minute till Midnight
133) I am not Okay
134) My body weak

Spring

137) Healing change
138) Winds of Change
139) Sinking heart
140) Crossing Paths
141) Field of flowers
142) Hope is
143) empty
144) Surgeons Table
145) Words on a Page
146) I Worry about You
147) IDK
148) Violent past and suns warm rays
149) Alone I pray
150) Closed doors
151) Soul fire
152) Who am I?
153) Oh pillow beneath my head
154) Feeling of Nature
155) Mad Hatters Well
156) A glance in the eye
157) God I'm Falling
158) Beauty in the fall
159) I want to believe
160) Always the poet, Never the poem

161) Tired soul
162) I am a book Unbound
163) Dream of a lost friend
164) You are my shield
165) Yearns for the moon
166) Calming from a Faceless Angel
167) Destiny
168) Watching her dance
169) It feels like nothing else matters
170) I wish that I could fly
171) Hold me like you love me
172) Broken heart of mine
173) Thoughts in the night
174) Shooting stars
175) Fireworks
176) Lifes concert
177) I listen to the music
178) When the music starts
180) I feel a change
181) Shining eyes
182) Random thoughts
183) Removal of thoughts and sound
184) I meditate
185) Inspiration in the night
186) Moon rises with beautiful melodies
187) I have an art
188) Flood of you
189) Poetry in your hair
190) glass boats
191) My forever missed
192) To My Mother
193) Dark gardens
194) If you were a flower
195) Masked illusions
196) Refractions
197) Waiting
198) Wanna hear my deal with God?
199) I'm Sorry My Friend
200) Curse of a Bleeding Heart
201) Trying to seal up my heart

202) Run and be free
203) Poems on my mind
204) I love Poetry
205) Raw soul honest and true
206) Shadow of hope

Summer

209) from beneath the mulberry tree
210) mid summer day dream
211) Calm, relaxed
212) Love
213) Eyes
214) Kissing you
215) Comforting kiss of fires flame
216) Beauty of the night fire
217) Sparks of love
218) Hidden Battles
219) Let our demons play
220) How can I know
221) I crave your presence
222) Funerals for the Living
223) Ghost of you
224) Bury me beneath the garden
225) Depression in the mind
226) The solder
227) The wanderer
229) Feelings you may never know
230) First thought last thought
231) My Friend
233) Blue eyes
234) Dear Ocean eyes
235) What is Happiness?
236) Hazel eyes
237) Pictures
238) Forget the world
239) If I could tell you everything
240) My bleeding heart
241) Just me and you

242) Hearts bleeding again
243) Touching eternity
244) The calm before my storm
245) Loves battlefield
246) Loves sacrifice
247) Scared afraid
248) Good night
249) Trance
250) Universe of love
251) My crazy family
252) A bronzed god
253) To My Friend
254) To the one I love
255) In the stardust together
256) Beautiful Little one
257) Tomorrow
258) I think I love you
259) Even if she falls
260) To the future one

www.ingramcontent.com/pod-product-compliance
Lightning Source LLC
Chambersburg PA
CBHW060149050426
42446CB00013B/2739